DATE DUE

NORMAN AND LILIAN RACK

MACRAMÉ:

ADVANCED TECHNIQUE AND DESIGN

DOUBLEDAY & COMPANY, INC., GARDEN CITY, NEW YORK   1972

To Mike

Acknowledgment:

Photography by Larry Songy
Advice by Bill Thompson and Joan White
Macramé by Gene and Ellen Andes,
    George and Rosemary Hoag and Betsy Milam
Drawings by Gene Andes

we are grateful

Library of Congress Catalog Card Number 72–175416
Book design by M. F. Gazze

What has become popular as macramé was known to the sailor as "square knotting," a relatively small part of fancy ropework used to make small decorative items aboard ship or small gifts for family and friends. The work being done in this field presently has gone far beyond the relatively restricted work of the early seafarers. Although we will present instructions for several projects in the modern style for those who wish to duplicate them, our main purpose is to encourage you to explore the unlimited possibilities of the craft. The serious craftsman will move quickly to designing in his own style rather than copying ours.

The last portion of the book will deal with more traditional areas of fancywork that may not be known to the person who has only recently discovered macramé and will show how these lesser-known techniques may also be adapted to modern design.

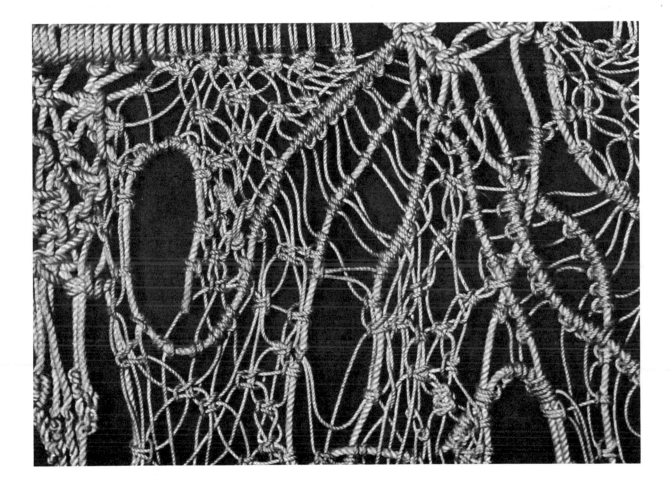

CONTENTS

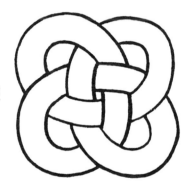

BOOK ONE

MACRAMÉ:
ADVANCED TECHNIQUE AND DESIGN

CORD *What Is Cord?*

There are many cords now available for use in ornamental knotting, and you should understand something about how cord and rope are made in order to choose the cord to use for a particular project. Each type of cord has properties that determine its appearance and working characteristics.

Ordinary rope is made by twisting together several yarns. The yarns themselves, are made by spinning, also a twisting process. The characteristics of the yarns, and of the rope, will be determined by the nature of the fibers used to make the yarn and the type of twist used in the spinning.

There are many natural and synthetic fibers being used to make yarn for the rope industry. The natural fibers include those of animal and vegetable origin. Certain of these fibers have become more commonly used in ropemaking than others because of their strength. At the present time, certain animal fibers are still being used to make yarn for the textile industry, but there are virtually no animal fibers being used to make rope and twine. Wool rug yarn may from time to time be useful in decorative knotting, but it is not the best choice because its fuzzy texture tends to obscure the knots in a knotted piece. The vegetable fibers, however, are still being used for rope and twine, although they have been largely replaced by synthetic fibers. The vegetable fibers you will encounter most often are cotton, linen (flax), and members of the hemp family of plants (hemp, sisal, and jute). Aboard sailing ships, until relatively recently, almost all rope was hemp, termed "Manila" by the sailor, because the best rope was that made from Manila hemp. There was also a smaller amount of cotton line to be found aboard the old sailing vessels, but its use aboard such vessels was limited. The cord sailors used for their recreational knotting was often of cotton, however, and this cotton line probably was the personal property of the sailors brought along for decorative knotting, or made aboard ship from scraps of cotton cordage or discarded cotton fabric.

If you fray the edges of a piece of cotton cloth or cotton twine until you can divide the fibers no further, you will have arrived at the basic unit from which rope is made. It was the ropes in the rigging of a ship which supported the masts, instead of the other way around, and it was the ropes of the rigging which worked the sails and positioned the spars against the force of wind and water, and thus the ancients who invented rope gave man the means to put to work for him those tiny fibers of the tough hemp plant. The secret of making strong cord from simple fibers is in the spinning process. Before the fibers are twisted into yarns, they are combed, or carded, to align the fibers in parallel, so that when the yarn is spun the fibers will not tangle and kink but lie as much as possible side by side. Kinked fibers will break, but fibers twisted together will not break and will have a strength related to the cohesion among them. Failure of the yarn will be due to separation or sliding apart of the fibers, not breaking. If the fibers in a yarn are parallel, the cohesion among the fibers becomes the determinant of the strength of the yarn. In twisted yarn, the fibers actually spiral tightly about each other with the result that a longitudinal pull on the yarn will slightly stretch the spiral, as when you stretch out a coil spring. This little bit of stretching decreases the diameter of the yarn slightly, causing a sidewise clamping effect on the individual fibers. Within limits, the greater the pull on the yarn, the tighter the grip of the fibers on each other. Also, natural fibers are irregular in shape with multiple tiny spirals, bends, and protuberances, and these microscopic irregularities cause the fibers to interlock further, essentially by snagging on each other. The smoother and more perfect the fiber, the more difficult it is to spin into sturdy yarn. The rough-textured fibers of flax, cotton, and hemp make strong yarns and ropes.

Simple spinning is easy; good spinning is very difficult. Sailors made what they called "spun yarn" by twisting cotton or hemp fibers in their hands or on simple spindles. This spun yarn was used aboard a sailing vessel for many of the tasks for which we use household twine. Rope and sailcloth were precious aboard ship, and a rope or sail worn beyond usefulness was never discarded but was patiently frayed into its component fibers and made into spun yarn.

It is not certain whether sailors may have made some of their own macramé cord by twisting spun yarn into twine,

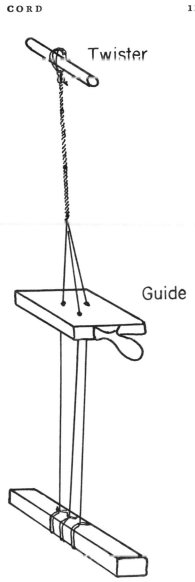

Simple rope-making machine. One man twists the end of the growing rope while a second advances the guide. Rope made with this machine will be 20–40 per cent shorter than the length of the starting cords, depending on the tightness of the twist.

but given the ingenuity of the sailor and the tedium of a long sea voyage, it is likely that they did. A simple ropemaking machine, like the one shown, could easily be rigged in the crew's quarters, or on deck, for the manufacture of cord. In the machine shown, there are balls of yarn or twine serving as source of component cords, and the cord from each ball is led over and under several wooden dowels to put tension on them. The twister is a handle to which the cords or yarns are fastened after passing through a guide. It is the twist applied by the twister that makes the rope. The twist of a cord must always be in the opposite direction to the twist of its component cords or yarns. If yarns are made with a clockwise twist, cord made by twisting these yarns together must have a counterclockwise twist. Rope made from these counterclockwise twisted cords will have a clockwise twist, and cable made from several ropes will be twisted counter-clockwise. (Directions are given as they would appear to a person standing at the guide of a ropemaking machine facing the twister. To the twister, the directions would appear the opposite.) If you wish to try making some homemade rope, you can make some by using the rig illustrated here. In this type of machine, this distance between the twister and the fast ends of the cord will shorten 20–40 per cent during the twisting.

As you may have concluded already, the ropemaker's answer to the need for stronger rope was to twist greater and greater numbers of cords together to increase the number of fibers in the rope. We have said that ropes may be twisted into cables that are twisted in the opposite direction to the twist in a rope. Sailors and informed laymen call the twist of any twisted cord the "lay" of the cord. There are, thus, "rope laid" cords in which the twist is clockwise and "cable laid" cords in which the twist is counterclockwise. Most cords commonly available will be rope laid. When viewed from the side, the cords of the rope will appear to spiral downward from upper left to lower right. Conversely, cable-laid cord will spiral from upper right to lower left.

In addition to the direction of twist used in making it, cord is also described by naming the number of component cords used in the final twisting. Most rope is "three ply,"

Twister

Guide

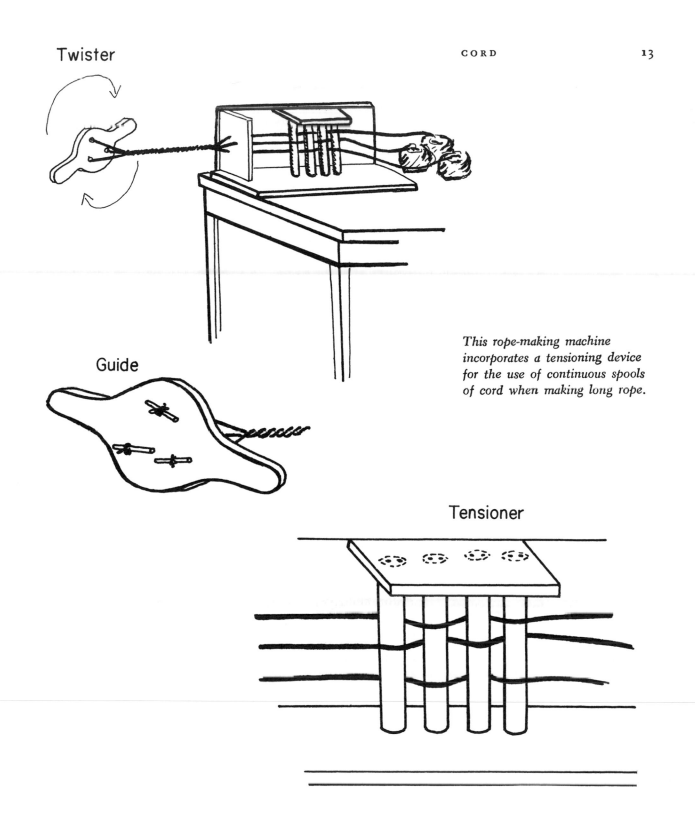

*This rope-making machine
incorporates a tensioning device
for the use of continuous spools
of cord when making long rope.*

Tensioner

that is, three cords were twisted together in the final step in making it. Although it is possible to increase the diameter, and thus the strength of a rope, by twisting together more than three cords, rope of more than four ply is uncommon, probably because of the difficulty of splicing cord with so many components.

Ordinary rope is generally three-ply, rope-laid cord. Formerly, the size of the rope was given in terms of the circumference rather than the diameter. The sailors "one-inch Manila" may be translated as three-ply, rope-laid hemp cord of one-inch circumference (about one third of an inch in diameter). At present, especially for smaller rope of cotton or synthetic material, the size is given as the diameter, but be careful when ordering from a marine supplier or ship's chandler, where the older usage may still prevail.

During the latter days of the sailing era iron and steel were used increasingly in the rigging of sailing ships. Steel wire provided the strength required to support tall masts under the load of the vast sail area carried by the later square-riggers. Hemp rope of equivalent strength was of such a large diameter that it was impractical. Ropemakers' development of techniques for making steel rope made possible the clipper-ship rigging. By the early twentieth century, most of the major supporting ropes of sailing vessels were steel. The ropes that were handled by the men and passed through the many pulleys of a vessel remained hemp, however, until later developments in the ropemaking industry made hemp rope nearly obsolete.

Hemp and cotton rot. This simple fact plagued sailors and ship builders for centuries. Some of the problems created for the sailor by the continual decay of rigging are mentioned in the later chapter on splicing, as well as some of his solutions to the problems.

With the development of the synthetic fibers, particularly nylon and dacron, the sailing man was at last provided with a strong rot-proof fiber for the making of rope. Because the synthetic fibers are more perfect than the natural ones, they lack the tiny irregularities that are so important in providing the cohesion among fibers spun into yarn. In other words, the synthetic fibers could not be spun, and their widespread use in rope had to await the development of processes for the manufacture of continuous fibers of indefinite length. Once these techniques had been developed, it was possible to make twisted rope that was stronger than hemp and would last years instead of months. Within a very short time, nylon and dacron cordage have almost completely replaced cotton and hemp rope.

Increasing interest in pleasure sailing and changes in sail and rigging design have resulted in the popularity of braided rope. This rope consists of a central core of longitudinal fibers covered by a round braid similar to those discussed beginning on page 104. This cord is less likely to foul in the gear of a sailboat and is much easier on the hands than twisted rope. Although generally more expensive than twisted rope, braided rope is used almost exclusively on the modern pleasure sailboat, and is called "yacht braid" by many sailors.

If there were no other cordage available, the knotting hobbiest would have a fair selection of cords from among the working ropes. The recent popularity of square knotting (macramé) has resulted in many other types of cord being made available. Many yarn suppliers now carry a line of several types of cord expressly designed for macramé. These cords are available dyed or undyed, and the occasional knotter will find it easiest to purchase his supplies from such a supply house. In the Appendix we have included a list of all the suppliers we know of for those who may wish to order their cord by mail.

The supply houses generally carry a line of cotton cord in a wide selection of colors, and they may offer cotton cord in several sizes. They also often have a similar cord in twisted nylon and, perhaps, braided cotton and nylon cord. Some very ornamental braided cords are available with metallic fibers in the braided covering, which are quite handsome. Also popular is twisted jute twine, either natural color or dyed. Almost any of the cords offered by these houses may be used for decorative knotting, but we have certain preferred types of cord that we use almost exclusively.

Perhaps because we have approached macramé from the tradition of nautical fancywork, we feel that almost all ropework looks best in the old-fashioned rope-laid cotton cord. Many of the synthetic braided cords are perfectly acceptable for use in macramé, but we find that highly ornamental cords, especially the metallic ones, detract from the knots. When such cords are used the attention is quickly focused on the beauty of the cord itself, rather than beauty of the patterns of knotting. The beginner is often tempted to buy this highly ornamental cord for use in macramé, but we would suggest that it is better to master techniques using simple twisted cotton cord, which is more readily available and much cheaper. Fancy cord does not compensate for sloppy knotting or poor design, and the most accomplished knotters very rarely use these fancy cords.

Most of the projects in this book have been made with nylon or cotton seine twine. Seine twine, also termed mason's twine, is three-ply, rope-laid cord available in sizes ranging from $1/64$ to $1/4$ inch diameter. The sizes are numbered and are relatively constant from manufacturer to manufacturer. The size number refers to the number of yarns in the cotton twine: Number eighteen twine is made from three cords each of six yarns, number twenty-four twine from three cords of eight yarns, number thirty-six from three cords of twelve yarns, and so on. Nylon seine twine is similar to the cotton but is twisted from nylon filaments that are finer than the cotton yarns. The cord manufacturers, however, have sized the nylon twine with numbers corresponding to the sizes of cotton cord. Seine twine is working cordage, not ornamental string. It will, therefore, be cheaper and stronger than most of the fancy cords available. It is available undyed by the pound, and may have a few bad spots in it, but its low cost and wide range of well-standardized sizes more than compensate for the bother of dying and cutting it yourself.

Cotton seine twine is sometimes still sold in three grades: hard, medium, and soft, named for the tightness of the twist applied during its manufacture. Medium-twist twine is best for general use, but people with delicate hands may prefer to use the soft twine. If you buy soft cotton seine twine, remember that the soft cord of a given size is of larger diameter than the medium twine of the same size, because the soft twine has been more loosely twisted.

This diagram contrasts rope-laid cord with braided cord.

The twisted cord illustrated is number twenty-four cotton seine twine. The braided cord shown has a central core of twisted yarns within an eight-part round braid. Small diameter braided cord intended for use where strength is not required may lack the center cord.

A few of the many cords available for use in macramé are illustrated in the photograph on the next page.

A

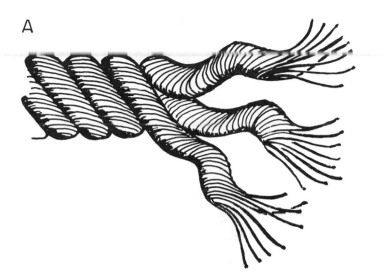

Twisted and braided cord contrasted:

A. No. 24 cotton seine twine (24 yarns) with counterclockwise twist. Eight yarns in each cord (clockwise twist).

B. Eight-strand round braid, central core of longitudinal fibers.

B

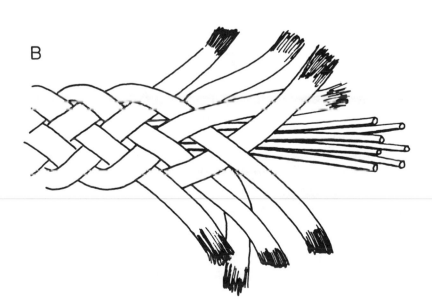

Cords used in macramé
(top to bottom:)

No. 12 cotton seine twine
No. 24 cotton seine twine
No. 36 cotton seine twine
No. 72 cotton seine twine
No. 120 cotton seine twine
No. 12 nylon seine twine
No. 48 nylon seine twine
No. 72 nylon seine twine
cable-laid nylon twine (Craft Yarns
   of Rhode Island "crinkle cord")
jute twine (American Thread Co.)
four types of braided nylon twine
   from various suppliers
solid braided nylon rope
   (curtain tieback)
¼ inch-diameter nylon rope
two-strand nylon rope
leather boot lace
¼ inch-diameter Manila hemp rope
⅜ inch-diameter Manila hemp rope

Both cotton and nylon seine twine may be dyed or stained easily to produce variety in color for your work. Some cord suppliers catering to persons doing fancy knot-work sell dyed seine twine in a wide range of colors. These suppliers necessarily charge more for the seine twine but often charge the same price for the dyed as for the undyed cord. If you purchase seine twine from such a house, you can get the colored cord at no additional expense. Also, a few inquiries at local hardware stores will almost always be rewarded with several types of twine suitable for your purposes. Ask for mason's twine, chalk line, seine twine, netting twine, postal twine, or kite string if you want twisted cord, or ask for venetian-blind cord if you want polished braided cotton cord.

We stain cotton cord with dilute oil paint or wood stain to produce several shades of brown and red. For clothing and many ornamental hangings, we use home-dyed twine. By dyeing our own cord, we can produce several shades of the same color, and we can custom mix our own colors. All our dyeing is done with Rit or Tintex dye. Dyeing equipment consists of several plastic dishpans and two enamel buckets for heating the dye solution on the stove.

Cotton cord takes the dye more easily than the nylon but is less colorfast, especially in the darker shades. Presoak cotton cord for several hours to remove any sizing or dirt before dyeing it. Most cotton cord is usually supplied in one-pound hanks, but if it should come wound in balls, unwind these for more maneuverability. Loosely tie each hank to prevent tangling and presoak the cord in the bathtub or sink using hot water and changing the water at least once during the soak. Recently, we have found that cord made from cotton grown in certain areas will not dye evenly, due to heavy deposits of oil-based defoliants used on the cotton plants just prior to harvesting. The cord manufacturer assures us that baking soda added to the presoak will remove all the oil. We add some detergent, too, and it seems to work.

Make up the hot- or cold-water dye according to the directions on the package in dishpans and transfer the soaked cord directly to the dye bath. Allow about thirty minutes to one hour for the dyeing, stirring frequently, then remove the cord from the dye and rinse it in cold tap water until the rinse water runs clear. Hang the cord outside to dry, or allow it to dry on thick pads of newspaper.

Nylon cord is dyed in similar fashion, except that the nylon requires higher concentrations of dye and longer in the dye bath. We often heat the dye bath gently on the stove when dyeing dark colors in nylon using enamel buckets to hold the dye. Also, since nylon twine is usually supplied rolled onto tubes, it is necessary to coil it into hanks and tie it loosely before dyeing it. Presoaking the nylon cord is not necessary.

Varnish will protect and preserve cotton cord. Pieces varnished after completion will take on the golden color of the varnish, which darkens slightly with age. In addition, ropework that has been adequately varnished may be washed with soap and water when dirty. We use marine spar varnish, exterior-grade varnish, or the newer polyurethane plastic varnish. The older varnishes are a deep amber color and tint white cord a golden brown, which will darken slightly with age and exposure to light. The plastic varnishes are clear, and white cord varnished with them will remain white. By varnishing different parts of the same piece with the two varnishes, some variety in color may be produced. Dilute wood stain may be applied to the unvarnished cord, or added to the varnish, to produce a brown color. If you thoroughly varnish a mat or braid, apply undiluted wood stain, and rub off the excess with a rag, an antique finish may be produced in which the coils of the cord are accentuated. After the stain has dried at least twenty-four hours, apply a final coat of varnish.

Because cord is so absorbent it will soak up varnish. At least six coats of varnish are usually required for the rope to be thoroughly protected. Using a small brush, apply the varnish liberally to the cord and allow the varnish to dry thoroughly between coats, usually twenty-four hours. Keep applying the varnish until the cord has a finish similar to that of the wood of your furniture. Varnish comes in high gloss, semigloss and matte finishes, so you must use the appropriate varnish for the finish you desire. But if you have varnished a piece with high-gloss varnish and decide that a matte finish would be better, just apply a final coat of the matte-finish varnish, and vice versa.

When cord has been thoroughly saturated with varnish it will be rigid, almost as strong as wood. If you have a three-dimensional hanging that will not hold its shape, you may prop it into the desired shape with small sticks and varnish it to make it rigid.

Because varnish accentuates the minute fuzzy fibers projecting from the surface of any cord, it is better not to varnish such cords as wool rug yarn, jute twine, or any of the many sisal twines. Cotton, hemp, linen, and nylon twines and ropes varnish nicely, and the varnish finish adequately weatherproofs those cords subject to decay.

Detail.
Wall hanging by Ellen Andes.
Home-dyed No. 72 cotton seine twine in seven-foot working lengths.
Ceramic beads by Bill Remington.

GETTING IT ALL TOGETHER

Tools

You will need something to measure cord and something to cut cord. Pictured in the photograph are the other tools (not all necessary) that we have found useful in reducing aggravation.

Other equipment useful for certain projects is discussed later on.

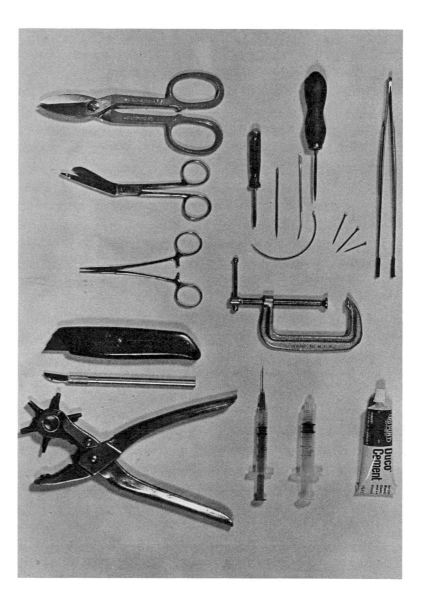

Tools for macramé
and nautical ropework

tin shears
bandage scissors
hemostat
utility knives
rotary belt punch
small screwdriver
needles:
        upholster's and sailmaker's
awl
large forceps
C-clamp
disposable syringes and needles
        for gluing
cement

How Much Cord to Cut

When you have decided on a project it is best to cut enough cord for the entire job before beginning. There is no good rule for computing the lengths of cord required for a macramé piece. The cords will have to be three to seven times the length of the finished piece, but the actual requirements are determined by the density of knotting in the pattern used, the size of the cord used, and the tightness of your knots. Even the experienced knotter often begins a project with only a general idea of what the finished piece will be like, so it may not be possible to accurately estimate the cord requirements for a given piece. For some of the simpler projects illustrated in this book, we will give the lengths of cord used. Once you have mastered several methods of adding cord to a work in progress, you will not worry about running short. As we will show, it is relatively easy to add on cords inconspicuously. Several of the elaborate hangings pictured were worked in short lengths of cord and new cords added at frequent intervals, so that the worker enjoys the ease of working with short cords, which are less likely to tangle, without limiting himself to small projects.

The easiest method of cutting large numbers of cords the same size is to place two C-clamps half the desired length apart and use them as posts around which to wrap the cord—or perhaps use the posts of a bed. Cut the cord at one clamp, and you will have a number of cords of uniform length—twice the distance between the clamps.

Cotton seine twine does not unravel very fast, so we often do not bother tying or gluing (with Duco Cement or white glue) the cut ends if we are working on a project that can be tied fairly rapidly. When using nylon cord, however, we find it necessary to tie overhand knots in the ends or melt the ends in a hot flame, because the nylon twine will unravel rapidly as the piece is tied. Most braided cords will not unravel significantly and do not need to be tied or glued. If you wish to melt the ends of nylon cord to secure them and you have not done it before, be very careful. Nylon catches fire at a relatively low temperature and burns with a hot flame, dripping globs of molten nylon on unwary knotters.

The very hot flame of a gas stove burner—don't use the burner from an electric stove—will suffice if you don't have access, as we do, to a small propane torch. If you use a torch, work over a large pan of water. A small hot flame will heat the nylon rapidly and fuse the minute fibers of the cord without blackening the nylon. Using a low, cooler flame, as a match or cigarette lighter, will cause carbonizing of the nylon so that the cord will turn black. Nylon fused with the hot flame of a torch will be discolored slightly to a yellow or brown, but the discoloration will not be noticeable if the fusing is done carefully. When finishing a piece after it has been tied, we heat the nylon similarly and have found that it is possible to fuse the ends without noticeably changing the color of dyed nylon cord.

Storing

Cutting cord is probably the most boring step in preparing to execute a project, so we often cut several pounds of cord at a time and store the extra to have ready when we feel the inspiration to do some knotting but lack the inspiration to do the cutting. If you plan on doing much macramé, you'd better organize a storage system from the start. Most of the people we know who have been doing knotwork have uncounted small- and medium-sized cardboard boxes partly full of half-completed projects and leftover cord. A better approach is to devote a corner of a closet or spare room to storage of cord and incomplete projects. Uncut cotton and nylon cord may be kept in small boxes until used. Dyed hanks of cord may also be boxed or hung from hooks on the wall. Never put the cut cord in boxes, except for transporting it. No matter how carefully you place the cord in a box, it will always tangle in the most incredible ways. Bend small S-shaped hooks from coat-hanger wire and use them to hang cut cord from a curtain rod or towel bar fastened to the wall about seven or eight feet from the floor. Arrange the cord by color and size, and you will be able to find the cord you need when you need it. Also, you will be able to design projects to use your leftover cord and will enjoy the double benefit of using your scraps while making projects without the annoyance of cutting cord. Restrict your cord buying to three or four sizes of cord of various colors, so that the remainders that accumulate will be of relatively uniform diameter and thus more usable than scraps of widely disparate size. You may also wish to save short lengths of cord in a box, but will probably find as we did that short lengths are rarely usable. We usually keep on hand cotton and nylon seine twine in sizes 24, 30, 36, 48, and 72, dyed and undyed, and several balls of novelty cord and braid. For the investment of twenty or thirty dollars and a few hours of time, we have a pallet of cord permitting us to rapidly execute a project in response to a new idea. Nothing deadens artistic inspiration more than long delays.

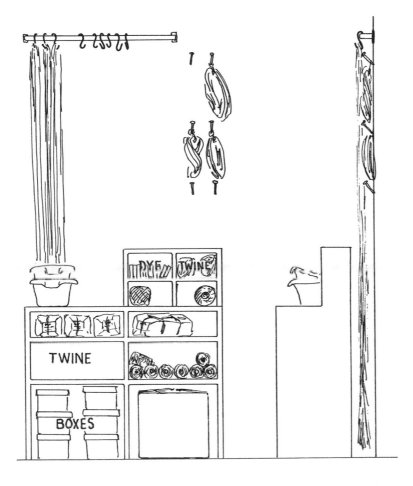

Storage plan. Home-dyed cord is hung in hanks from nails or pegs and precut cord is hung with hooks from a wall-mounted curtain rod or towel bar.

Square-knotted purse with wooden beads by George Hoag.

Beads, Bells, and Things

Many things may be incorporated into macramé projects for aesthetic or technical purposes. Beads, bells, rings, and rods have been popular with knotters for some time, and several suppliers now carry very complete assortments of this sort of accessory. When choosing objects to use as adjuncts to your knotting, remember the intended use of the finished article. For example, there are many painted wooden beads that are attractive but not suitable for use in a piece exposed to the elements, as a patio hanging, or to rubbing wear, as a purse or wristband. Unfinished redwood beads, however, are relatively weatherproof and do not have a surface finish to rub off.

Since most beads are designed to be strung on fine thread, the holes are very small—too small to pass most of the cords you will be using. Wooden beads may be adapted to macramé by drilling the holes larger, but glass and ceramic beads will break if you try to drill them. At present there are several suppliers who carry beads designed for use in macramé and these beads have larger holes which pass medium-sized twine easily.

Ceramic beads sold for macramé are usually made especially for each supplier by local potters so that the size and shapes available will vary. With few exceptions, the holes in these beads are huge, and will easily pass No. 72 cotton seine twine. The shapes and colors available are limited only by the imagination and patience of the potter. If you know of a potter in your area, you may ask him to made some beads or clay shapes for you, or you could make the beads yourself and have him fire them for you. Making beads is tedious work especially when making many beads of matching size and shape, so expect that handmade ceramic beads will be somewhat expensive. There are low-fire clays on the market now that can be fired in the kitchen oven, but we have had no experience with them since we get ours from a local potter. You may wish to experiment with making your own beads using this clay, but we doubt that the time and cost involved will make it cheaper for you to make simple beads. It would probably be better to buy the simple

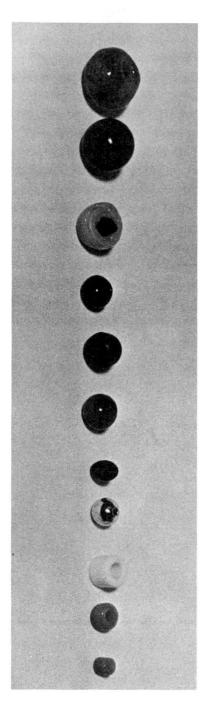

Beads suitable for macramé. A tile bead is pictured on the bottom with a crow bead just above it. (Courtesy Sun Shop.)

beads you need and reserve experimentation for custom shapes or odd beads not otherwise available.

Most glass beads are too small for use in macramé, but we have found two commonly available types that are large enough to use. Tile beads are tubular glass beads about ¼ inch in outside diameter and ³⁄₁₆ inch in length. The hole will easily pass No. 36 cotton seine twine, and No. 42 can be forced through. Crow beads are rounded glass beads with an outside diameter of ⅜ inch and a length of ¼ inch. The hole in these beads will easily pass No. 42 cotton seine twine, and two strands of No. 42 cotton twine can be forced through. Both the tile beads and the crow beads come in a wide assortment of colors. The crow beads have a shiny surface, the tile beads have a matte or dull finish. Both of these beads are shown in the photograph together with some other beads which you may be able to locate.

We have made some hangings with bells in them and would advise that you be sure to buy solid brass or copper bells. The widely distributed brass bells made in India are very satisfactory, though expensive, and come in many shapes, sizes, and tones. Cheap chrome-plated jingle bells from the dime store soon rust, but good quality harness bells, when they can be found, will not only sound better, but also last longer.

Rings are very useful for tying circular hangings, and may also be used for belt buckles and purse closures. Whenever possible, buy solid-brass rings. Hardware stores and saddle-repair shops—as well as most of the mail order cord supply houses listed in the Appendix—usually have a good selection of rings from half an inch to three inches in diameter, and stock only the solid-brass rings. Some stores carry brass-plated steel rings, which are to be avoided because the brass plating is very thin and will wear off rapidly exposing the steel which will rust. The same is true of rings and buckles with the so-called "gilt finish." If you must use brass-plated steel or plain steel, paint the articles with a rust-preventing oil-base paint or clear plastic varnish before incorporating them into a piece that will be exposed to wear or to the elements.

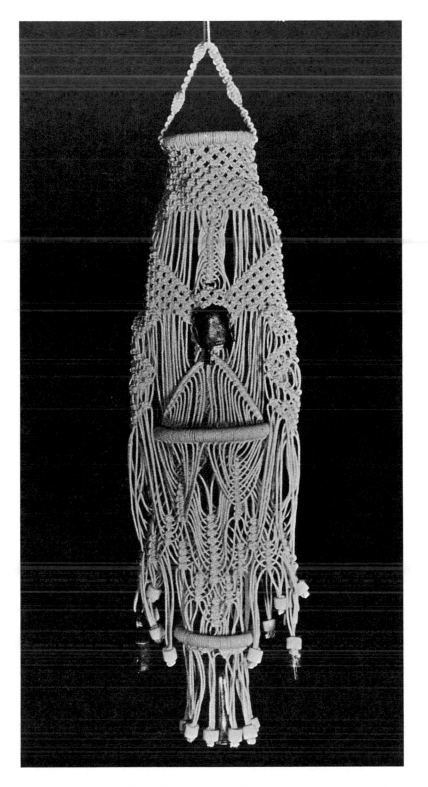

*Hanging with bells by Ellen Andes.
No. 24 cotton seine twine, undyed,
in seven-foot working lengths.
18 inches high.*

If you wish to use rings larger than three inches in diameter, or metal supports of other shapes, you will have to make your own or have them specially made for you. We use brass or bronze welding rod to make special wire shapes for hangings. You can use coat-hanger wire, but it is steel and subject to rust, especially since bending it will cause the protective painted coating to chip off. Welding rod comes in many sizes from $\frac{1}{32}$ of an inch to $\frac{1}{4}$ inch in most of the alloys commonly available, and each rod is thirty-six inches in length. Most towns have a supplier of welding equipment who will probably be able to provide suitable rods for your use. Be sure to tell him what you want to use the rod for, because many supply houses will have a bin of odd lots, or rod of unusual composition, which may be cheaper. Get plain rod without the flux coating. Thin welding rod, up to $\frac{1}{8}$ inch diameter, is easily bent by the hands or with a pliers into the desired shape. If you use pliers to bend the wire, wrap the wire in an old rag so that the pliers will not scratch it. Thin rod may be cut with a pliers, a heavy wire cutter, or a metal saw. When we make a ring, we braze or weld the joint to close the ring. Similarly, other complex shapes may be built up by brazing rods together. Since most homes lack welding equipment most people solder the welding rod using ordinary lead solder and a small propane torch or soldering iron. Brass rod, in particular, solders very easily although the grayish-white solder seam will show against the yellow of the brass. If the rod is to be completely covered by the cords of the project, the seams may be made with plastic or cloth tape or with wrapping of fine copper wire. We haven't tried epoxy glue or any of the various metal-mending plastic compounds, but there is no reason why they couldn't be used to fasten the rods.

Larger diameter welding rod, up to $\frac{1}{4}$ inch in diameter, makes fine straight supporting rods for flat hangings. It is cut with a metal saw and the sawn edges filed and sandpapered smooth. Regardless of the shape you have made of welding rod, polish the rod with fine steel wool and apply a protective coat of clear plastic varnish or lacquer to all parts of the rod that will be exposed in the finished project. It is probably a good idea to polish and coat the entire metal piece if the hanging is to be used outdoors, because the coating will minimize the corrosion of the brass. Corrosion of brass is less a problem than rusting of iron and steel, but it does occur and the greenish corrosion may stain the cords of the hanging. We occasionally use uncoated brass in a hanging of natural cord and allow the gradual corrosion of the brass to color the cord a delicate green.

If you have trouble finding brass welding rod, you may be be able to locate large copper wire to use instead of brass. The cautions for brass apply also to copper, but the main disadvantage of copper wire is its high cost.

Steel wire may be used for hangings if you wrap it well with plastic tape or paint it with rust-preventing paint. We have never done a piece in which the rust was deliberately allowed to color the cord, but there is no reason not to. Perhaps a hanging with brass (green corrosion) and steel (reddish corrosion) in it would be attractive. The problem with corrosion in iron and steel is that the rusting process does not stop at the surface but will continue until the piece is completely decayed away. Although it may take decades for a thick piece of unprotected steel to completely corrode, thin steel wire may disappear with alarming rapidity. Brass, bronze, copper, and aluminum, on the other hand, develop a surface layer of corrosion which serves as a barrier to further penetration of oxygen, preventing corrosion of the deeper layers of the metal.

Because of its light weight, softness, and anti-corrosion characteristics aluminum should be an ideal metal for use in macramé designs. We have not used aluminum because it is expensive and cannot be welded or soldered easily. If you do not wish to solder your metal frames, aluminum may be the metal of choice. It can be joined by riveting or wrapping with tape. Also, there are several special glues designed for this purpose. Aluminum wire, rods, tubes, framing, molding, and sheets may be found in most stores handling materials for the home craftsman or do-it-yourselfer, and the sales personnel in such stores should be able to assist you in deciding how to fasten the aluminum together.

For unusual projects, you may wish to use other metals for framework. In the color photograph of the compass stand the framing was done with galvanized steel pipe, the pipe that plumbers use. If you should want to make something in which the frame must support a heavy weight, this pipe may be purchased from a plumber or large hardware store cut to length and threaded for the appropriate connectors. At some additional expense, you could have the frame assembled by a local plumber, but be prepared for some strange looks when you show him a sketch of the frame. This pipe is very strong, and the galvanized coating (zinc plating) will effectively prevent rust. There are few projects, however, that would warrant the expense and weight of this material.

For many of your projects, wood will be the material to use for making frames and supports. Although not as strong as metal, wood is lightweight, inexpensive, and readily available to most knotters. The wood you use may be a dried branch or a piece of driftwood, or it may be commercial lumber cut and fashioned for a specific project. You can find dowels of various sizes and many patterns of molding at the lumberyard, which will be very handy for starting supports for flat or three-dimensional hangings. Many department stores have wooden curtain rings and large-diameter wooden curtain rods that are available plain or painted various colors. The rings will have a small screw eye on the outer edge which may be removed before using the ring in a hanging. Unfortunately, curtain rings come in one size only, so you will have to use metal rings or make your own rings if you need other sizes. Embroidery hoops come in round and oval shapes and although expensive may be satisfactorily used in hangings. If you have a power jig saw or saber saw, or have a friend who has one, you can make the most incredible shapes out of thin plywood for use in hangings. Old chair legs or bannisters make attractive turned wooden pieces for use in hangings. If you wish, they may be cleaned and refinished or antiqued for a most elegant appearance.

Although we use all of the above means to find materials for use in macramé, our major method remains scrounging. An occasional visit to the salvage yard will provide objects—junk to some—that may be transformed by a little work into *objets d'art*. In New Orleans, several demolishing companies maintain large sheds and yards full of objects salvaged from demolished houses which are a scrounger's delight. The several marine salvage yards and government surplus houses are a similar experience. If you are not near a junkyard, or hesitate to spend a day prowling through heaps of junk, try browsing in a large hardware store. The incredible variety of small pieces of hardware will certainly suggest projects to you.

Perhaps the single handiest hardware item we have discovered is the wire lampshade support shown in the photograph. These frames are available in three sizes up to ten inches in diameter and make wonderful large-diameter rings for circular hangings. In addition, cords may be hitched onto the three spokes of the frame and used to make a design in the center of a cylindrical hanging. When making lamps, we attach the socket for the bulb to the center hub of the frame.

Metal parts useful in hangings:
lampshade rings
curtain rings
brass harness rings
oval sail thimble
fishing swivel
brass bells

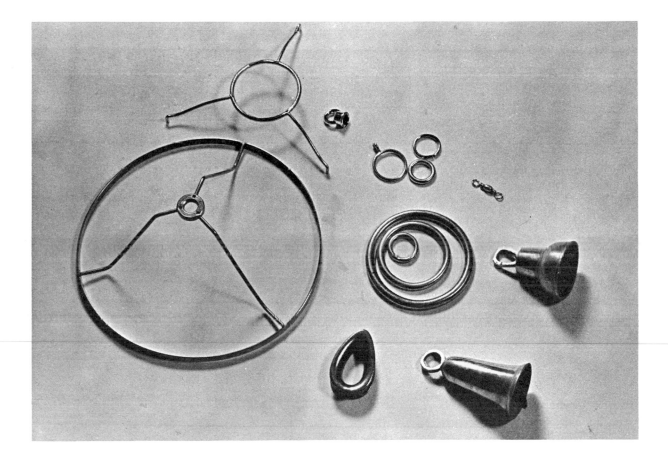

Hanging lamp in dyed cotton seine twine by Ellen Andes.

Most of the lamps in the photographs were made using various sizes of these frames. The appliance service shop where we buy the frames also carries a good stock of ornamental glass globes and chimneys with the appropriate bases for them. With the frames and globes, it is a simple matter to make the lamps illustrated. You may find it difficult to locate some of the more specialized items we have used for the lamps, but ask your hardware dealer to let you check his catalogues of spare lamps parts and then special order them. If you don't have any luck, write Meynier's Appliance Service, 7911 Maple Street, New Orleans, Louisiana 70118, and I'm sure they will be able to help you. You may also want to buy inexpensive lampshades at the local department store, remove the shade fabric, and use the frames as we have suggested. Or simply macramé a new fabric with which to recover the shade. Some of the ornamental mats and braids we will present later may be glued directly onto a lampshade and the entire shade varnished to make a nautical-style lamp for the den or bar.

Found objects, such as seashells, rocks, corks, broken glass, and metal junk, may also be used in hangings, but it is necessary to stockpile several boxes of junk to have on hand a reasonable selection. We have some friends who vacation frequently on the Florida beaches and have provided us with beautiful seashells for hangings. In the area they visit, many of the scallop shells have been nicely drilled for us by oyster drills, which make a round hole, about ⅝-inch, in the base of the shell. Without the services of the oyster drill, you may find it difficult to drill seashells and will probably do better to simply tie them into your hanging.

When choosing objects to include in your hangings, remember to be cautious about corrosion and deterioration of the material. The proud owner of your work may have later cause to regret your haste in buying or using certain articles.

Because macramé has become so popular lately, many supply houses now offer a selection of articles for use in hangings. Do not rely on the judgment of the seller, who may be unfamiliar with macramé techniques and who cannot be expected to know your intended use for the articles you may buy. Be sure to check that the rings you buy are solid brass and the ceramic beads, if unglazed, are weatherproofed. We have found that the better-quality articles are in the long run cheaper than the inferior grade.

Ornamental mats and braids may be used to decorate small wooden boxes. (Pages 93, 98 and 129.) Suitable boxes may be found in the decoupage department of a large store or at one of the decoupage specialty shops, but it is often possible to find better-made boxes at the hardware store or dime store for about half the price. Since the box surface may be entirely covered by the ropework, you could use a cigar box, but if you do, be sure to varnish it thoroughly *both* inside and out, because the contraction of the glue and varnish used to fasten the mats may warp the cardboard.

When using fancy knotwork to make decorations to be applied to tables, boxes, picture frames, and bottles, we fasten the cord with Duco Cement or white glue. Be sure to use them with caution, for if they are dropped onto cord to be dyed, stained, or varnished, the pigment will not penetrate the cord at those points, and the finished piece will be uneven in color. When gluing mats and braids to a surface, be careful that the glue reaches only the back of the mat or braid. In cases where a braid or mat must be cut, we use glue to prevent the collapse of the rope work at the cut end. The ends so treated must be used in designs that permit other rope work to cover the area glued. This is why small mats cover the corners of the tables and the picture frame shown on page 132.

Macramé

In the first appendix we have provided a glossary of knots. The basic knots used in macramé are ancient, and all have perfectly good names by which they have been known for centuries. Some recent writers have ignored these names and used or suggested others, perhaps in an attempt to simplify the learning of knots. In our glossary we have included most of the knots you will be using and have attempted to clarify the confusion in nomenclature which may exist. It is not necessary to know the name of a knot in order to tie it, but it is in order to tell another how a specific project has been executed. Please refer to the glossary so that our usage will be clear to you.

The essence of macramé design is not the knowledge of many knots, but rather the ability to combine the several basic knots into pleasing patterns.

There are several patterns based on simple knots which will be useful again and again as you plan and execute macramé projects. We prefer to categorize them according to their principal uses and, thus, will present (1) starting patterns, (2) working patterns, and (3) finishing patterns. A complex project may be broken down into combinations of these three types of patterns. The best practice pieces are flat hangings. These range from wall hangings to room dividers, but in all cases they are essentially two dimensional structures. As you progress to more elaborate hangings and macramé constructions, you will be designing in three dimensions, but may approach them as combinations of two-dimensional structures.

After a discussion of the principal patterns we use in hangings, we will show some other useful techniques and then some finished articles that illustrate the ways these patterns may be combined into designs.

Starting Patterns

Most macramé hangings are begun by hitching the cords over a rigid support. This support may be a wooden

Cords are attached to the wooden handle of the purse with lark's head knots.

dowel, metal rod, leather tab, or almost any other object as those discussed previously. Cords are usually hitched onto a support with the *Lark's Head Knot.* This knot may be combined in several simple ways to produce decorative edges for the start of a piece, as illustrated. The same patterns may be used along the sides of a piece, as you will notice in some of the projects illustrated in this book. When tying clothing —such as ponchos, vests, or dresses—we usually begin at the top by hitching the working cords over another cord, which serves as the support piece as well as the outline of the project.

When the lark's head is used to attach cords to a support, the cords are doubled and, therefore, their length is halved. If you estimate that you will need twelve-foot cords to execute a hanging, cut your cords 24 feet long to obtain twelve-foot working cords. Doubling the cords also means that you will always be working with an even number of cords. If the piece planned will be mainly square knotted, start with a number of cords that is a multiple of four so that the square knot row will reach all the way across the piece and will be easily centered. For example, a piece that is 40 cords wide will be 10 square knots across with 5 knots on each side of the center line, and a piece 44 cords wide will be 11 square knots across with the middle knot on the center line. A piece 42 cords wide, however, will be 10½ square knots wide with 5 and ¼ knots on each side of the center line and thus not easily centered. Designs can be made symmetrical only if you have a good center line.

The particular starting pattern you use may be determined in part by the patterns you wish to use later in the piece.

For example, when a spacer cord is used to tie lark's heads between the cords being attached, as shown in the diagram there will be two turns, or loops, around the support for each working cord set up. When clove hitches (see below) are tied over a support, there are also two turns around the support at each working cord. These two patterns, the lark's head with spacer and the clove hitch, may therefore be tied close together, as shown in the diagram without any differences in spacing.

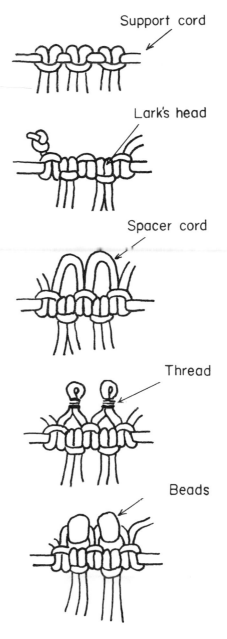

Support cord

Lark's head

Spacer cord

Thread

Beads

Using lark's head knots to hitch cord to a starting support.

Lark's head with spacer cord followed by a row of clove hitches. Note that the horizontal distance covered by each pattern is the same.

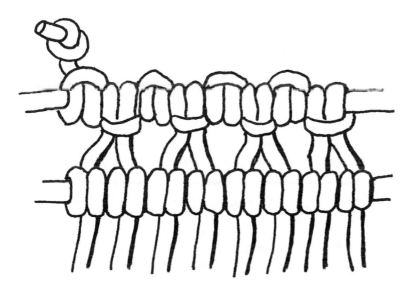

Working Patterns

The *Alternating Square Knot* is a pattern useful for making flat pieces—such as clothing, screens, or room dividers—where a relatively dense pattern of knots is desired. This pattern may be tied closely or openly as shown. The number of knots tied may be increased as in the diagrams here.

The number of knots in each row of the alternating square knot pattern may be increased. Doubled and tripled knots are shown.

Square knotted headband in fine cotton seine twine by Rosemary Hoag.

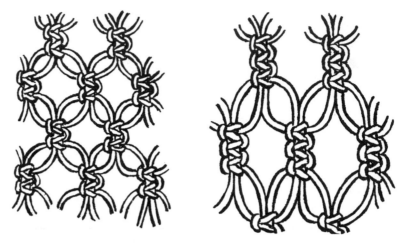

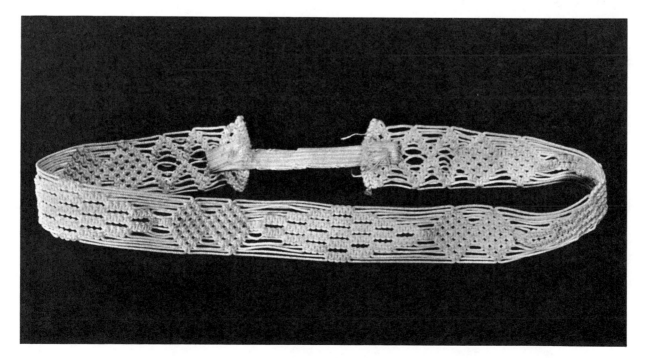

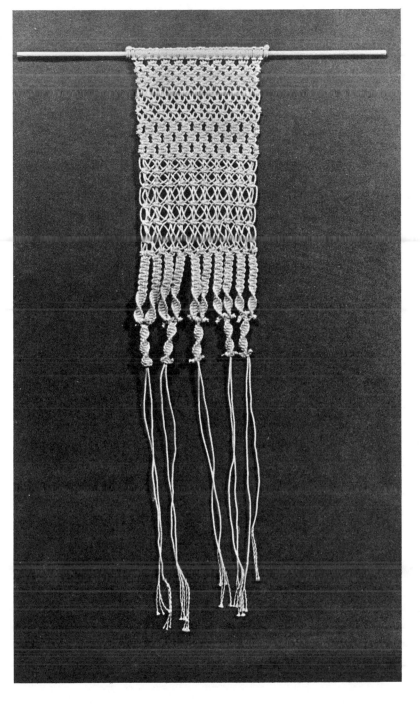

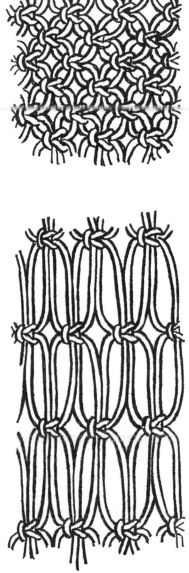

Square knot sampler tied to determine the gauge for the dress on page 72.

Alternating square knot pattern may be tied loosely or openly.

A simple variation of the alternating square knot is the *Basket Weave Pattern*, a good pattern for covering a lot of distance quickly while still producing a fairly dense network of cords. It is an alternating square knot pattern in which every other row of square knots has been replaced by simple over- and under-weaving of the four cords. Single and double basket weave is illustrated here. This technique of weaving may be used to make designs in other ways, especially when working in the alternating square knot pattern. The diagrams on this page show some simple variations of square knotting made by weaving the cords.

Single and double basket weave patterns are tied by replacing one or two rows of square knots in the alternating square knot pattern with simple interweaving of the four cords. (below)

Using the principle of weaving
the working cords to make
patterns in a field of alternating
square knots. (left)

Macramé pouch by Ellen Andes
in the basket weave pattern.

The *Clove Hitch* must be tied over a support. It is useful when tying rods, dowels, or wires into a hanging and is also used to make patterns. The sailors devised many clove hitch patterns by hitching over cords held horizontally, vertically, or diagonally. Several of the reference books on knotting have many illustrations of this type of design. We have shown a few in these diagrams.

As you can see in the photograph on the right clove hitching may be combined with square knotting in many ways to produce densely knotted designs or open, lacelike patterns.

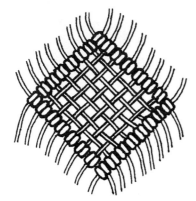

Clove hitch patterns. The designs are made by using one or more of the working cords as a support cord over which the other working cords are clove-hitched.

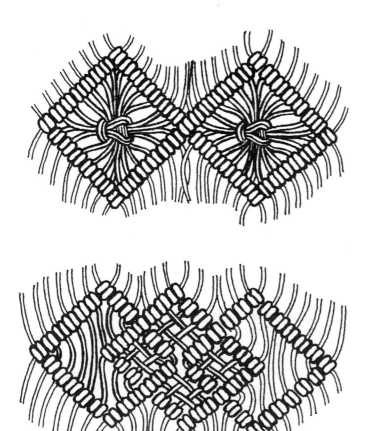

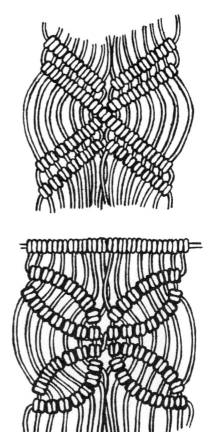

Wall hanging in jute twine by Betsy Milam.

The *Alternating Lark's Head* pattern is illustrated in the diagram. Double, triple, and quadruple alternating lark's head patterns are shown. Although very good for narrow pieces, such as belts and straps which must be strong, it is much too time-consuming for use in wide hangings.

The alternating lark's head pattern. The triple alternating lark's head is shown on the left, and the double and quadruple patterns are shown below.

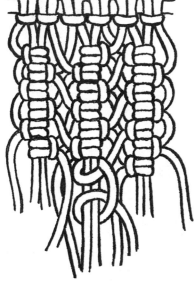

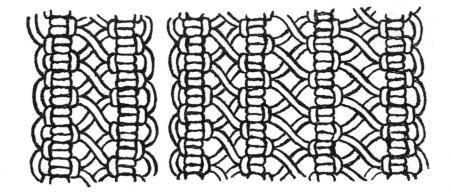

Square knot sennits. The right- and left-hand square knot sennits are shown in the left two illustrations, the left- and right-hand spiral (half knot) sennits in the middle two, and the reversing square knot sennit with a multiple-cord sennit in the right two.

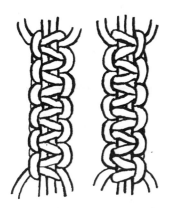

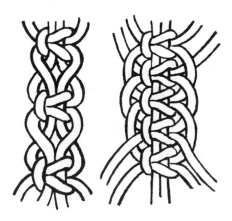

Narrow bands of knotting or braiding are termed *Sennits*. Several of the articles pictured use square knot sennits with good effect. Six types of square knot sennits are shown in the diagrams to the left.

Square knot sennits in illuminated hanging by Gene Andes.

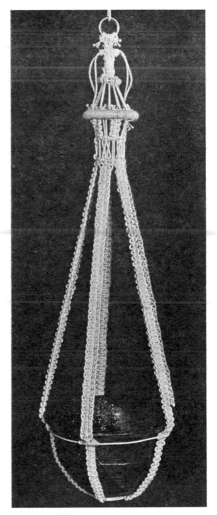

Hanging planter using square knot sennits. Pot by Bill Remington.

Finishing Patterns

Often as a work is in progress, you will wish to eliminate cords from the pattern. The simplest way to remove cords is to take them out of the pattern as fringe. If you don't want the fringe to show on the front, the cords may be pulled out the back of the work and trimmed close so the ends will not show. If the cords to be removed are at the edges, they may be left as fringe or trimmed short. At the edges or bottom, the ends may be woven back into the pattern and hidden, or sewn to seam binding and turned up in a hem.

Cords may be removed on the front or back of a piece by using them to tie one of the stopper knots, as explained in the section on nautical ropework that follows.

If a piece ends with a row of clove hitches, you can trim the cords close to the knots and glue them, as in the diagram.

Cords may also be threaded through countersunk holes in a wooden bar and knotted. The knots will fit into the countersunk part of the holes and may be glued or hidden by covering with wooden plugs or wood putty. This is a very handy way to end wall dividers or windowscreens that have a wooden frame.

Glue

Finishing a working pattern by clipping cords close to knot.

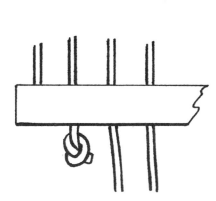

Finishing work by clove hitching over a dowel or passing the cords through countersunk holes in a wooden bar.

Lamp in undyed cotton seine twine by Gene Andes. 16 inches diameter by 60 inches high. (left)
Lamp by Ellen Andes. Undyed cotton seine twine, 10 inches by 36 inches high. (right)

Hanging planter of natural jute and wool yarn by Ellen Andes. (left)

Lamp by Ellen Andes. (right) Undyed cotton seine twine and home-dyed dacron braid. 24 inches diameter by 30 inches long.

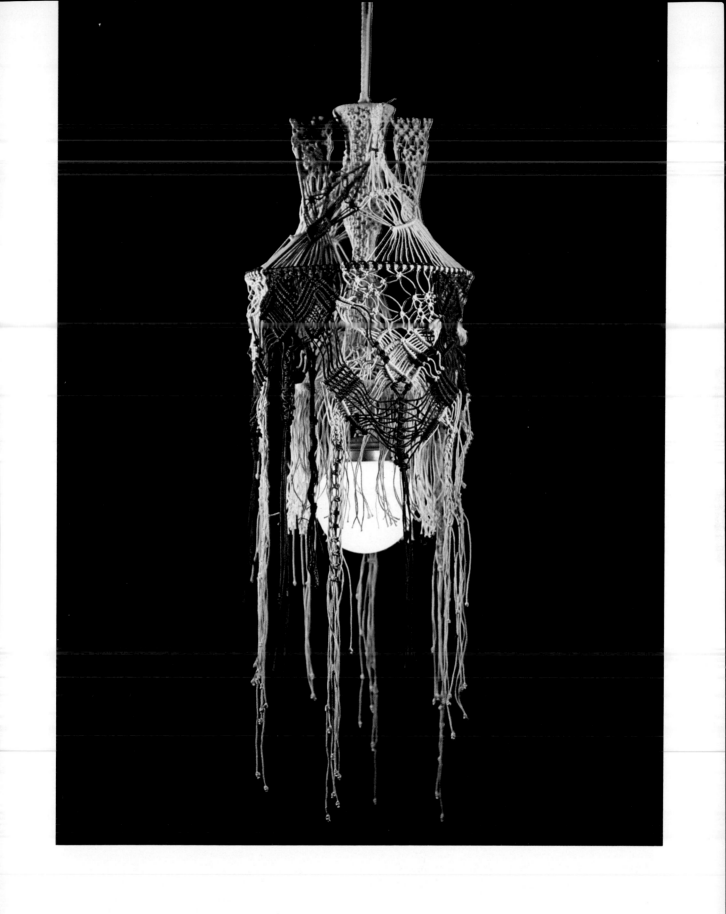

Lamp in dyed cotton seine twine by Ellen Andes.

As you have already discovered, cords often run short before a piece is completed. Short cords may be replaced in several ways.

The first method of replacing cords, shown here, replaces two cords at a time. In this method, the first half of a square knot is tied over the cords to be replaced, the new cord is doubled and hooked around the old cords, and the second half of the square knot is then tied over the two new cords. The cords that have been replaced are thus taken out on the back of the piece and may be overhand knotted and trimmed short, woven through the backs of several successive rows of knots and cut short, or simply securely glued at the point where the new cords were added and cut close after the glue has dried. The particular method used to finish the cords depends on the nature of the article being made.

When working in alternating square knots, two doubled cords may be threaded through the loops between two adjacent rows of square knots, and the added cords used to replace short cords, to increase the number of working cords or to tie an overlying ornamental knot or pattern on top of

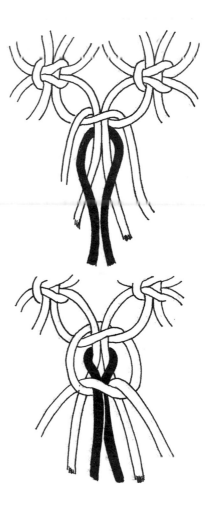

Replacing cords that have become too short when working in alternating square knots. The first half of the square knot is tied over the old cords, and the second half over the new cords.

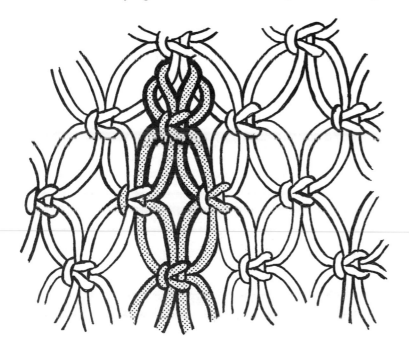

Adding four cords to the alternating square knot pattern.

Four cords added to a field of alternating square knots and used to tie an ornamental knot overlying the basic pattern.

Adding two cords by tying onto two old cords with a square knot.

the square knot background. (Illustration above.) This particular trick is our favorite method of increasing the number of working cords in a piece and it adds cords in groups of four, which maintains the number of working cords as a multiple of four when working in a square knotted pattern.

Cord may also be added by using the new cord to tie a square knot over two old cords (diagram to left). Notice that this method adds two cords at a time rather than four at a time.

Cords pulled out of the working pattern to form a square knot sennit overlying the piece, then those cords reworked into the working pattern once again.

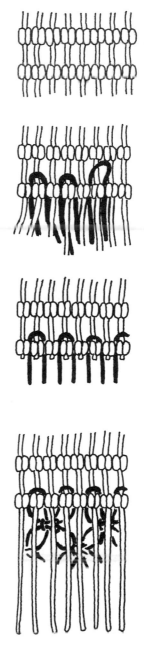

Changing to cords of a different color or making a row of fringe. This technique is particularly useful when making fringed or multicolored garments.

To change colors when adding new cords, tie two rows of horizontal clove hitching about ¼ inch apart and thread the new cords through the spaces between the rows of clove hitching. The old cords may be trimmed close to the lower row of clove hitches and cemented, or may be taken out of the pattern as fringe overlying the new cords. This last method is useful when tying fringed clothing as it makes fringe at the same time it changes the color of the cord you are working with.

With practice, you will no doubt develop other methods

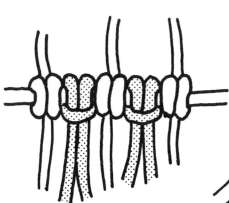

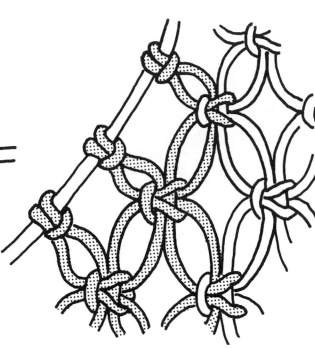

Adding cords to a work in progress with the lark's head. (above) The example to the right is commonly used along the edges of tapering or fitted garments.

Decreasing in the alternating square knot pattern by deleting four cords at a time as fringe.

Ⓕ point at which cords are deleted.

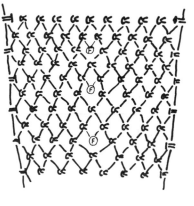

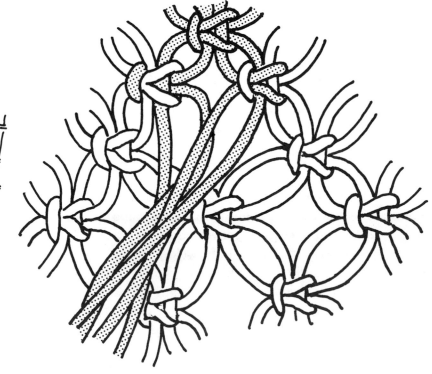

of adding cord to replace short cords or to increase the number of working cords. These are some of the ways that the lark's head may be used to add cord to a work in progress, and can be particularly useful for making tapered sides of garments, as when working the armhole of a dress or increasing in a flared skirt.

When making a fitted garment or shaping a three-dimensional hanging, the methods of adding cords we have mentioned are very useful. For example, if you begin a circular hanging by hitching thirty cords over a three-inch metal ring, work two rows of alternating square knots and double the number of working cords by adding, according to the method mentioned on page 49, between every knot in the second row of square knots. In this way, the piece will flare abruptly. The number of cords added and the rate at which they are added will determine the rate at which the diameter of the piece will increase and, thus, the shape of the piece.

To make a circular hanging curve inward to the center, the diameter is decreased by decreasing the number of working cords. Similarly, a flat hanging or garment may be made to taper to a smaller width by deleting cords.

Cords may be taken out of a work by many means. The most direct method is to tie them off at the edges and trim them short or use them for fringe. This method is used in flat hangings and clothing, but is not suited for a cylindrical hanging in which there are no side edges. When working on a circular hanging, in which we wish to decrease, we first do a few rows of alternating square knots, closely tied, and then delete cords four at a time at several places around the circumference of the circle. As with the increases, the rate of decreasing determines the curve of the tapering piece. The cords to be deleted are usually taken to the inside of the hanging and glued and trimmed close, but occasionally we bring them out on the outside of the hanging and use them to make fringe or tassels.

You will soon discover other methods of deleting cords which the particular hanging you are working on will suggest to you. In all your work, let the project suggest new things to you and never hesitate to drastically alter your working plan part way through a project.

DESIGN

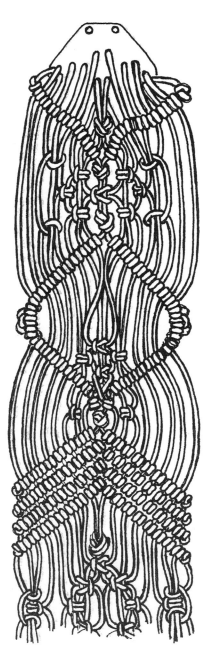

Good macramé design cannot be taught, it can only be learned, preferably from a person or book not imposing any system of design upon the student. The best macramé designs are usually spontaneous products of people flexible enough to learn from the knots and materials they are using without attempting to impose upon themselves, or their work, any limitations other than the natural limitations of their talent and the character of their working materials.

Despite that lengthy admonition, we will attempt to provide a general guide for the serious student who wishes to explore the possibilities of fancy knotwork.

If you haven't done much macramé, make a few simple belts or other short projects until you are sure you have mastered the knots. We have seen too many knotted pieces in which the basic knots have been so badly tied that it is amazing the entire thing didn't fall apart. As you do your practice pieces, concentrate on tying the knots tightly and evenly. Even the most stable of knots will not hold shape or position if tied loosely. Do not use any of the various clamps, belt hooks, or other holding devices now being sold as essential for macramé. Learn to tie all the basic knots "in the hand" as the sailors say; learn to tie them with cords free in three-dimensional space, standing on your head if necessary. Too great a reliance on clamps, hooks, clipboards, or tying boards will effectively prevent you from learning to design in three dimensions later. If you are making a belt, attach the cords to a ring or buckle, hook the buckle over your toe, and tie. You will find the distance between your toe and your hands easier to adjust than any of the clamps you may have seen. Tie belts using all of the basic patterns we have shown and make up patterns of your own. Tie belts with eight cords, tie belts with forty cords, and tie belts with every sort of cord you can lay your hands on. Use natural cord and dyed cord. Tie belts of one color and tie belts of many colors. Only with practice will you learn to correctly gauge the cord requirements of the various patterns, and soon each project will teach and suggest more.

The differences between belts and wall hangings are two: the width of the piece, and the degree of freedom possible in your design. Tie flat hangings until you tire of them, using every possible pattern you can think of. Each project will suggest others to you. Glance briefly at the belts and the hanging detailed in these diagrams and on page 56, and see if there are ideas there for you to use. Do not copy these projects but use them as a jumping off point for other designs. Avoid macramé patterns that appear in books or magazines unless the designs offer some new idea to you. Steal the idea, use it, change it, but don't copy the design unless you wish your wall to carry a reproduction of another's work, a reproduction that will probably be found in suburban living rooms from coast to coast.

After you have mastered the various basic techniques in your practice pieces, you are ready to go on to advanced design in three dimensions. There are two major areas of three-dimensional design. The first is best termed macramé constructions and includes three-dimensional pieces which may be hanging, standing, or, perhaps someday, crawling. In general, these articles are considered within the arty sphere of crafts design, probably because so many of them are strictly ornamental. We have attempted to show several examples of this type of construction that have practical use. Although we call them macramé lamps, they might be termed by some, "internally illuminated macramé constructions."

The second area of three-dimensional design consists of those items of everyday use that have been rendered works of art. In other words, if you have to have a particular something, such as a piece of clothing, you might as well have an attractive one. When undertaking projects of this type, the designer takes on certain limitations and problems that limit the freedom of his choice of design, but he enjoys, in the successful design, the double satisfaction of solving the problems while producing a thing of beauty. Andes' *Practical Macramé* is a good basic instructional text. Although most of the articles presented in it are clothing, the many solutions to design problems are useful in other projects.

So really, you must learn macramé at your own rate and in your own way if you are to achieve the proficiency in design that you desire. Having learned the basic vocabulary of knots, you need to keep only one rule in mind: there are no rules—if it has knots, it's macramé.

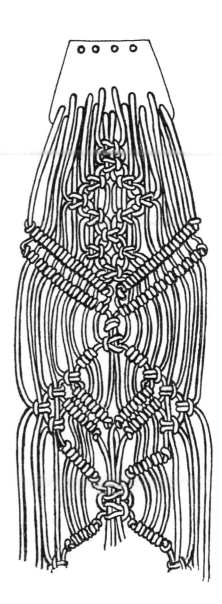

Tying diagram for two belt patterns, (above and opposite) using leather as clasp. Only the first half of each belt is shown.

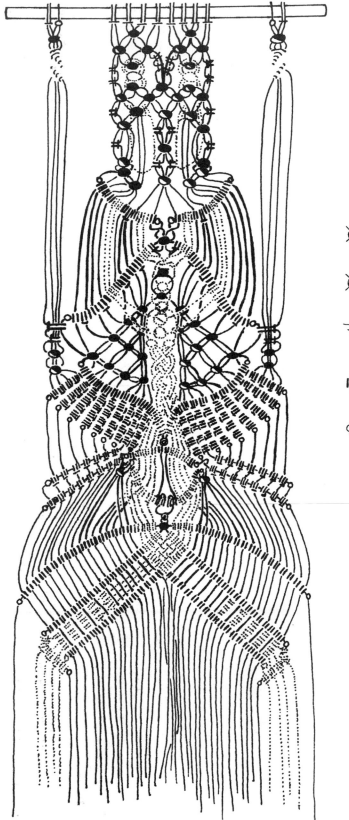

Typing diagram for hanging that appears in the color section.

| | left-hand square knot |

| | right-hand square knot |

| | lark's head |

| | clove hitch |

| | overhand knot |

Hanging by Gene Andes.

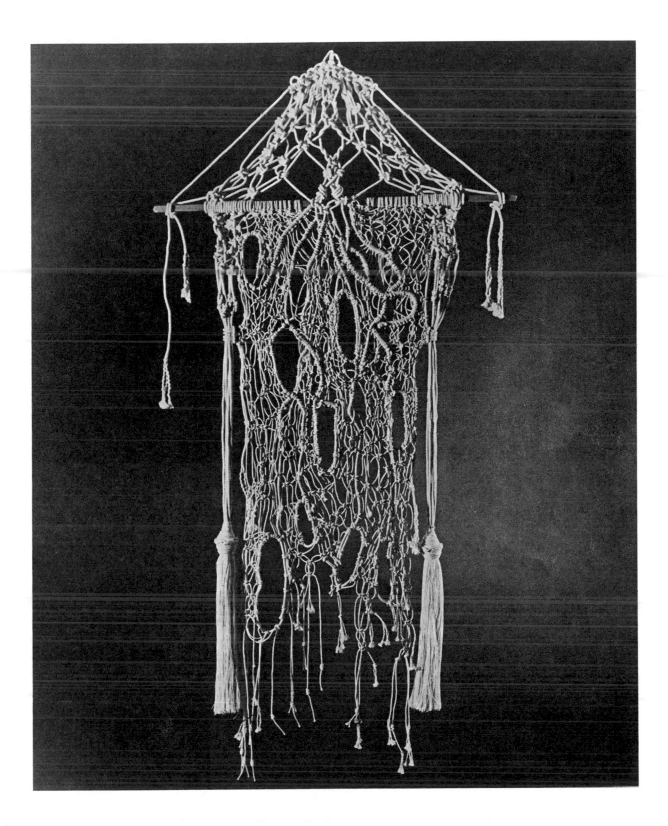

ORNAMENTAL KNOTS

From time to time you will wish to use some fancy knots in your designs. After you have learned to use the basic knots to design in three dimensions, there are some easily learned knots that may be used to advantage. The two most popular ornamental knots are the carrick bend or Josephine knot, and the Turk's head.

The *Carrick Bend or Josephine Knot* is the simplest of interlocking knots and is diagrammed here together with several of its principal applications. Notice that it may be tied with a single cord or with two cords. The carrick bend is the parent knot of a series of mat knots. Matwork will be discussed later, but for now a mat may be defined as a knot that is flat. There are mat workbooks, which are collections of the designs evolved over years from a few basic patterns. We will present a beginner's selection of mats later on. Mat knots are usually made two or three ply with multiple passes of the cords around the pattern, as we have shown. Our diagrams will usually show only the first passage of the cord; it is understood that any mat knot can be made two or three ply as we have shown on this page.

Carrick bend (Josephine knot) shown tied single and double ply. The drawing on the right shows the round carrick bend mat.

Turk's Head is a general term for another family of knots that are useful in macramé hangings. The basic Turk's head is easy to tie even for a beginner, but the more elaborate Turk's heads give an expert trouble. In principle, Turk's heads are braids tied with single cord that makes multiple passages around a cylindrical support. They are essentially closed circular braids. The braids will always be of an uneven number of cords—three, five, seven, and so on—and the number of cords in the braid is referred to as the number of "parts" when naming the Turk's head. The simplest Turk's head is, thus, a three-part Turk's head.

The Turk's head is a three-part braid in which two strands cross each other with one strand always on top, and the third strand weaves through the other two to lock the knot. In a Turk's head, the two strands that make the crossings will always cross an uneven number of times. When describing a Turk's head, the number of these crossings is given as the number of "turns" in the knot. The simplest Turk's head is now a three-part, three-turn Turk's head, and instructions for tying it are given on page 60.

Three-strand braid, which is the basis of the Turk's head.

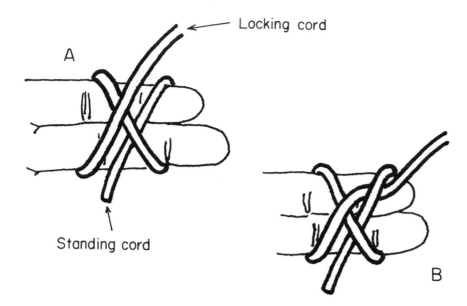

Locking cord

A

Standing cord

B

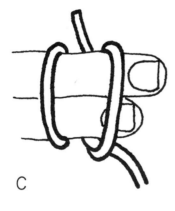

C

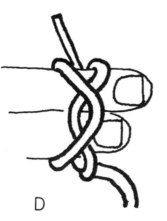

D

E

Tying the three-part, three-turn Turk's head in the hand. Note that the locking cord makes two passes and ends on the same side it began.

F

Locking cord

Standing cord

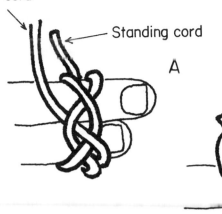

A

B

C

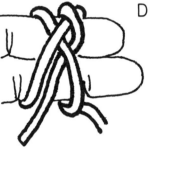

D

E

F

Increasing the number of turns in a Turk's head. Although the diagram presents the method of increasing a three-turn knot to a five-turn knot, the same process may be repeated to further increase the number of turns. The locking cord first passes over and under to the right, and then it passes over and under to the left, for each increase to be made. The locking cord always ends on the same side it began.

G

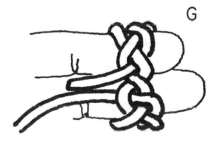

The three-part, three-turn Turk's head is too simple a knot for many applications, since when tied over objects of large diameter, there will be too few crossings or turns. Fortunately, increasing the number of turns in a Turk's head is much easier than increasing the number of parts. To tie a five-turn Turk's head, tie the three-turn knot, then lift over the crossing cord one more time and make two passes with the locking cord to stabilize the knot as shown on page 61. Seven-, nine-, eleven-, etc. turn Turk's heads may be tied by repeating the above process for the desired number of turns. Notice that the locking cord must always end up on the same side as the standing end of the cord in order for it to follow around again when tying two- or three-ply knots.

As a rule you will find it easiest to tie the Turk's head in your hands as we have shown, place it where desired, and then tighten it.

Turk's head sling used to mount souvenir cannon ball.

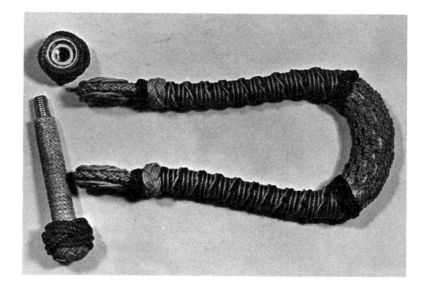

Sea chest handle covered with fancywork. The core of the handle is built up from rope and twine. The cross pin is a large bolt and rope-covered nut.

Searching through any of the knotting encyclopedias will produce quite a number of very complex ornamental knots that may be of occasional use. Don't bother memorizing any of these knots, for you will rarely use them. Tie them from the book when you need to use them. Some of these knots are so complex that they must be tied on a tying jig. If you choose one like that, be sure to save the tying jig for the next time you want to use it.

Tassel making is a special area of macramé worthy of a separate volume, but the principles of making simple tassels may be easily grasped and useful in your work. Tassels are bunches of fine fringe tied onto heavier, usually ornamental cord, with the juncture being overlaid by ornamental knotwork. You will find the Turk's head particularly useful when making tassels. The construction of several simple tassels is diagramed here.

Simple tassels. After the fringe has been secured to the basic cord by wrapping tightly with sturdy cotton or linen thread, the shape of the tassel is built up with cotton cord or tape and given a final covering of thin cotton or silken thread. The ornamental knots are tied in the hand and fastened to the tassel with glue.

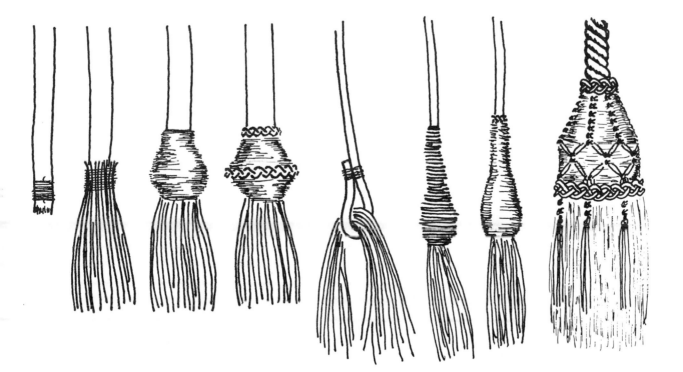

Fringe

Fringe may be as ornate or as simple as you desire. The simplest fringe is made by trimming the cords to uniform length and allowing them to unravel.

An *Overhand Knot* or the *Figure-of-Eight Knot* in the ends of the fringe cords will prevent unraveling, the ends of the fringe may be coated with glue to prevent unraveling.

Figure-of-eight knot

Overhand wrap knot

Nylon fringe may be fused with a torch, as described earlier, to secure the ends.

The *Overhand Wrap Knot* and the *Pear Knot* are variations of the overhand and figure-of-eight knot and may be used if you want a large knot on the end of fringe. These knots may also be used to tie several knots on a single long fringe piece or to tie a bead with a large hole onto small-diameter cord.

Pear knot

Overhand knot

Beaded fringe is easily made and quite handsome on certain articles. Crow beads and tile beads are most commonly used. Here are several examples of beads incorporated into a fringe.

Medium and heavyweight cotton seine twine is ideal for making stopper knots and back splices as fringe-ending knots. We will show you how to do these in the nautical rope work section.

Spanish-style fringe is made by using groups of fine cord to tie overhand knots. (see below)

Using beads in fringe. The lower drawing shows a design in long fringe made by tying in beads at different levels. A similar design could be made using wrap knots or pear knots in place of beads.

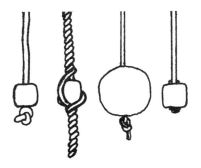

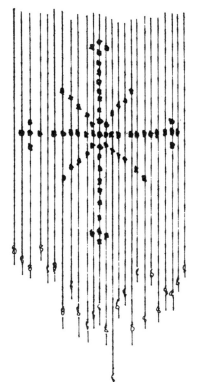

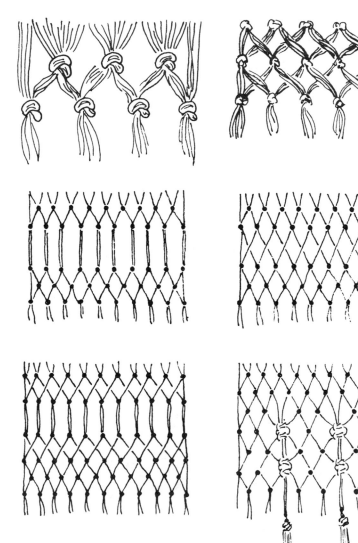

Flat circular designs are usually begun in the center and worked outward, increasing the number of working cords as you go in order to keep the piece flat. Here I've shown several methods of starting circles. The methods of adding on cord mentioned earlier are used to make the necessary increases as you work outward in concentric circles.

Hangings that are cylindrical or conical are fairly easy to do if you begin with rings as supports. Try sketching your idea in advance. It makes work on a complex piece easier and helps you visualize any modifications that occur to you while

CIRCULAR DESIGNS AND THREE-DIMENSIONAL HANGINGS

Several ways to start a circular pattern.

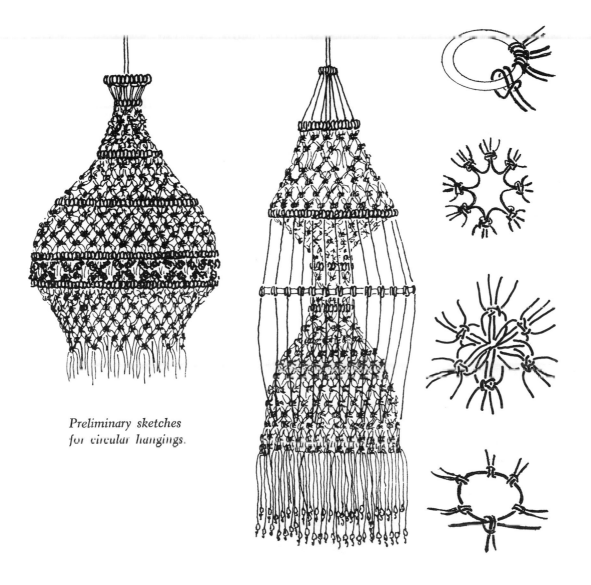

Preliminary sketches for circular hangings.

knotting. Several of the designs photographed were planned and executed in this fashion.

Square, rectangular, triangular, or irregular shapes may be used as supports in hangings, (a bent coat hanger, a frame-like structure made from wire or wood or plastic, many common household objects).

Usually complex dimensional projects are planned and tied as combinations of simpler two-dimensional subunits. In elaborate hangings, the framework may be assembled and the pieces tied in one operation, but it is easier to tie several components separately and assemble them after completion. The large hangings illustrated were tied in this stepwise fashion. The elaborate lamps and circular hangings were tied using wire frames for lampshades as supports; the frames were then bolted together to assemble the completed work.

You may use any size or type of cord in any pattern for macramé hangings. There are no rules to follow. Your designs are limited only by your imagination and the availability of supplies. If you have mastered the material we have presented so far, you should be ready to tackle some of the fancy hangings illustrated in the photographs.

Hanging by Ellen Andes. Undyed No. 30 cotton seine twine. This hanging was tied in three parts, assembled, and varnished.

Illuminated hanging by Gene Andes. Undyed No. 30 cotton seine twine in seven-foot working lengths. Several layers of cords were required for this five-foot-long hanging containing two lights.

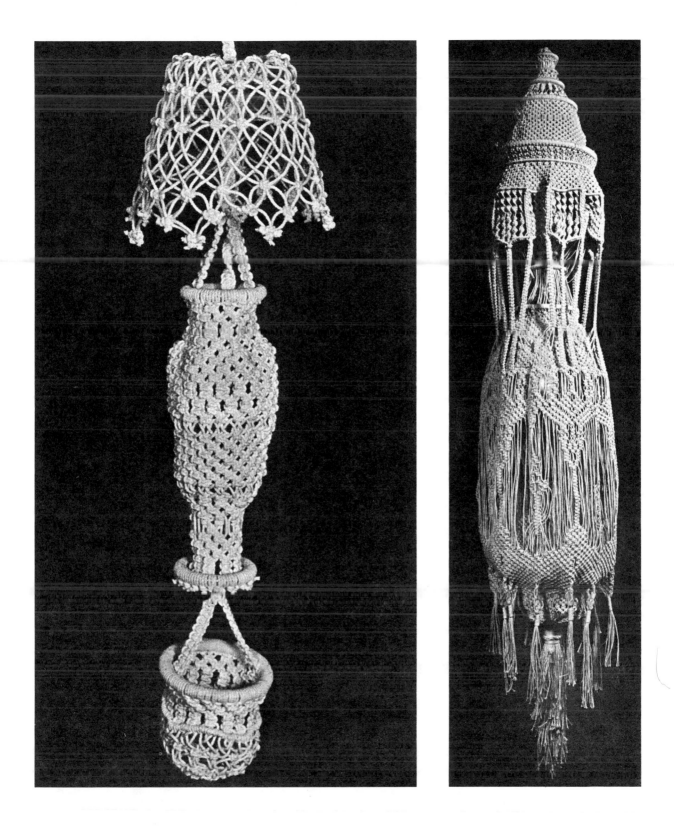

CLOTHING

Macramé is as easy to use for clothing as knitting or crocheting, and with experience goes faster. Because macramé is knotwork and machines can't tie knots, macramé clothing designs cannot be duplicated by machines—no one at the party will be wearing the same thing as you.

Unfitted garments, such as ponchos and capes, are the easiest to start with. A simple *poncho* is made by tying two rectangles in the pattern of your choice, perhaps a simple basket weave, and then joining them short side to long side. Fringe may be added for a more decorative border, as in the poncho below.

To make a poncho tie two rectangles measuring
14 inches × 26 inches (Small)
18 inches × 32 inches (Medium)
22 inches × 36 inches (Large)

and then attach the short side to long side.

Square knot poncho with multi-color fringe.

Ponchos may also be tied as square or circular pieces with a hole in the center. These are started in the center and tied outward, usually ending in fringe. The photographs on this page are of a somewhat more elaborate design based on the same principle.

Poncho patterns may be modified into cape patterns by leaving a front opening. Capes may be tied as circles or as partial circles. If you wish to have a full cape, use a circle pattern but remember to use fine flexible cord lest the finished piece be too stiff to drape properly.

Poncho by Gene Andes. Undyed No. 30 cotton seine twine in seven-foot working lengths. Tile beads used around neckline.

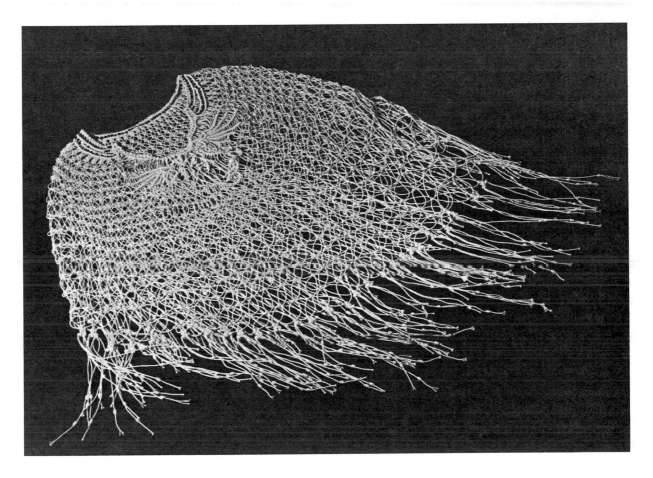

A skirt is also easy to tie. Use a sewing pattern or make your own pattern from muslin or paper as a guide to the shape of the finished piece. The skirt may tie at the waist only or may tie at several points along the side. Select or make a pattern and transfer it to a tying board. Run a single cord across the board for the waist band, hitch on working cords, and tie down, increasing the number of cords as you go to make the skirt flare. Lace the seams together to finish.

Fitted garments, like dresses or pants, are more difficult to design and tie properly. There are two approaches to use when tying a *dress*. The first method is to use a dressmaker's form, or a willing model, on which the article is tied directly. If you use this method, remember to leave seams or closures so that the finished article can be removed from the form on which it was tied.

The second method is somewhat more complicated in the designing, but easier to tie. It also is more flexible and of more general application. By adapting a sewing pattern into a macramé pattern you can use the macramé pattern to tie the garment in pieces that can be joined by tying. To make a dress by this method, select a simple pattern of the proper size and use only the pieces necessary for the outer shell of the dress. You will not need linings or facing pieces. Trim the pattern pieces along the *seam* line and lay them flat on a table or the floor. Measure the length of the bustline, waistline, hipline, and hemline, the length of the shoulder seams and neckline, and the distance from the neckline to bustline, bustline to waistline, waistline to hipline, and hipline to hemline. Use these measurements to draw a full-sized or -scaled pattern as shown in the diagram. As the dress is tied you will be making increases and decreases in the number of working cords to cause the piece to curve to fit the body. These increases and decreases will show slightly in the finished dress and are, therefore, best made either at the edges, where they will not show, or along lines that will become part of the pattern. This illustration shows the increase and decrease lines. For most patterns, there will be a few increases as you work from the neck to the bustline, a series of rapid decreases from the bustline to the waistline,

Macramé dress by Ellen Andes. Undyed No. 30 cotton seine twine in fourteen-foot working lengths.

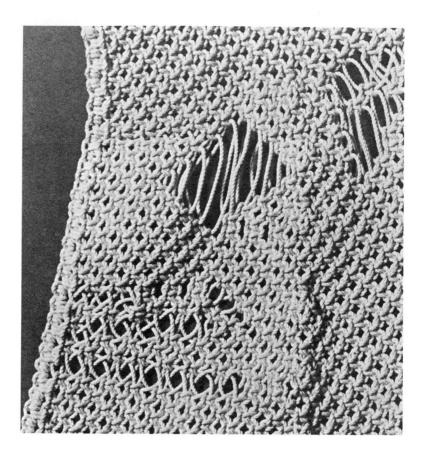

Detail of dress to show the line of increases in the front of the skirt.

and a second series of increases from the waistline to the hipline. These increases and decreases take the place of darts and gores in a sewing pattern, so when adapting a sewing pattern to macramé, you may ignore darts and gores and compensate by decreasing or increasing the number of working cords.

The dimensions of the macramé pattern is converted to numbers of cords and knots. Decide which knot patterns you wish to use in the dress and the type of cord you desire, and use some of the cord to tie a sampler of the patterns you will use. The sampler should be about one foot wide and long enough to include all of the patterns you wish to use. The sampler for the dress appeared earlier on page 41 and is made with No. 30 cotton seine twine which was used for the dress. By measuring the sampler, you can convert the number of horizontal inches to the number of cords, and the vertical inches to the number of rows for each pattern.

For the sampler pictured, there are 20 cords per three horizontal inches and 5 rows of alternating square knots per vertical inch. Each knotter's gauge will be slightly different, so it is necessary to determine your own characteristic gauge rather than relying on the figures we used in our pattern. Use the gauge conversion factor to convert the dimensions of your pattern to macramé dimensions. For ease of computation and of tying, round the number of cords off to the nearest even number. After the pattern has been completely converted to macramé dimensions, it is glued or taped to a tying board and small nails are placed along the outline of the piece to secure a single outline cord. The working cords will be hitched onto the outline cord using the lark's head with a spacer cord (see Working Patterns section). In the pattern illustrated, the bustline desired was 16 inches for the front piece and 14 inches for the back piece, which we converted to 212 cords based on the sampler. We sometimes round off the number of cords to a multiple of four because there are four cords in a square knot, and we usually use the alternating square knot pattern in clothing. For the front piece of the dress illustrated, we decided to begin with 18 cords on each shoulder seam and 32 cords along the center of the neckline, increasing to 120 cords at the bustline by adding cords along the side of the armhole and at points indicated in the drawing. Decreases were made from the bustline to the waistline by taking two sets of four cords out along the decrease lines of the pattern three times. There were 96 cords at the waist. The pattern was then increased to 160 working cords at the hemline, adding cords along the increase lines of the pattern. The back piece was tied similarly to the front except that the abrupt decrease from the bustline to the waistline was not necessary. We used 18 cords to start at the shoulders, 72 cords at the waistline, and 168 cords at the hemline. The front and back were joined by lacing a cord through the loops of the spacer cord as when lacing shoes.

Once you have converted a basic sewing pattern to a macramé pattern, it is possible to change the size of the pattern by converting the intended wearer's measurements to the appropriate number of cords and adjusting the pattern

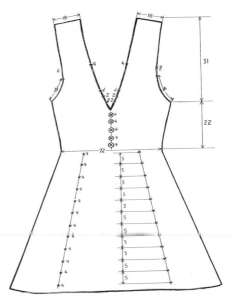

Macramé dress pattern front. This pattern was adapted from a size 8 sewing pattern and fits a size 3 or 5 petite. × = increase the specified number of cords. ⊗ = decrease the specified number of cords.

Macramé dress pattern back.

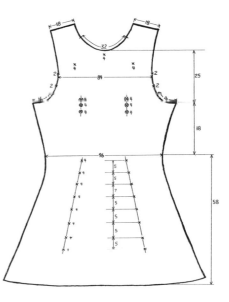

accordingly. The dress illustrated is based on a size 8 sewing pattern, and could be made larger by increasing the number of cords along the bust, waist, and hiplines. Adjustments for height must also be made when changing a pattern size, so you will need the distance between bust, waist, and hips when adjusting a pattern.

With practice you should be able to use the method described to make patterns for more complex garments, such as pants and dresses or tunics with sleeves.

Macramé can be used to make the upper portions of sandals, slippers, moccasins, and boots. Cotton cord used for footwear must be rot-proofed with an oil-based preservative, such as neat's-foot oil, or it will deteriorate rapidly. Linen cord will be more durable, but also more expensive.

For most of the articles you may wish to make, you will have to use leather for the soles, because cord soles will wear too rapidly. There is a special type of leather prepared for use as soles in footwear, and most leather suppliers will carry it. The leather is thicker and harder than leather intended for lighter uses and comes in several grades. Buy the best sole leather you can afford, as the cheaper grades will not hold up. To punch holes for the cords in the sole leather, you will also need a hole punch of the appropriate size for the cord. A rotary belt punch may do for making smaller holes, but you will probably need to use a large single-hole punch for thicker cord. The hole punch is driven through the leather with a mallet or hammer, using a scrap piece of leather as a backing. If you punch leather on a wood or metal backing, you will dull the hole punch after a few strokes.

The best way to construct your footwear is to use two layers of leather for the sole. The cords are threaded through holes in the upper layer only—the ends of the cords frayed, opened out, and pressed up against the upper sole. Then the two layers of leather are glued together with leather glue and short shoemakers' nails. The ends of the cord are thus securely glued within the two layers of leather as shown.

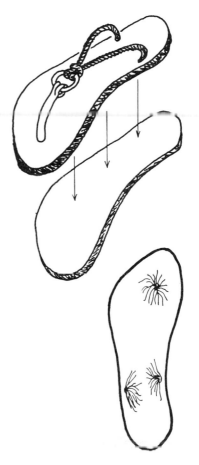

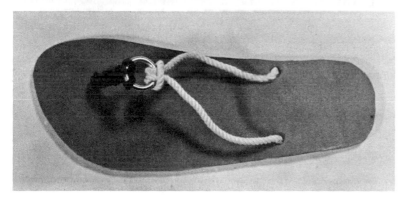

Construction of sandals. The cords of the straps pass through holes in the upper sole only and are secured by unlaying the cord and gluing the yarns between the layers of the sole.

Finished sandal.

To make the soles, trace your foot onto the sole leather and use a leather-cutting knife, or razor knife, to cut out two matching sole pieces for each foot. When you cut the second piece for each foot, trace the first onto the second with a pen facing the two rough sides of the leather together. When the two layers of each sole are joined later, only the good sides of the leather will show. Although the resulting double-thick sole looks fine for *sandals*, you may desire a thinner sole for slippers or moccasins. To make a thinner sole, make only the lower layer of the sole from sole leather and use softer thinner leather for the upper layer. It is the thinner upper layer that will be punched to receive the cords.

There are, of course, many patterns of knotting that may be used for sandal straps. We have shown a few in this diagram.

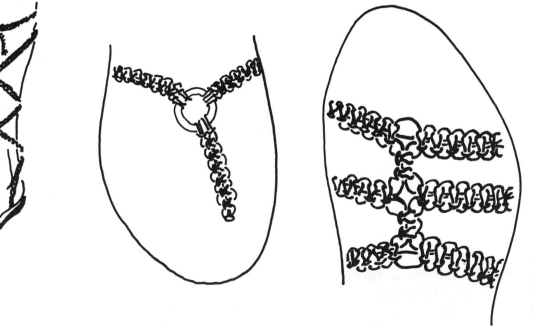

Three suggestions for simple sandal strap patterns of square knot sennits.

Slippers, moccasins, and boots have more elaborate tops, but the attachment of the cords to the sole is similar to that of sandals. Shaping the knotting is somewhat difficult, but can be done using some of the methods of adding and deleting cords which we discussed earlier. As you work on such a piece, make frequent fittings to be sure it will be a comfortable fit. You may begin this kind of footwear by passing doubled cords through holes in the upper sole and work upward, ending the piece in fringe, as shown. Or you can start at the top, without fringe, and work down, ending by passing the cords through the upper sole and gluing the ends between the layers of the sole, as you did in the sandals, see page 77. As in any macramé piece, things such as rings, buckles, and bells may be incorporated into your work, but be sure to place them so they will not rub the foot, particularly the bones of the ankle, heel, and instep.

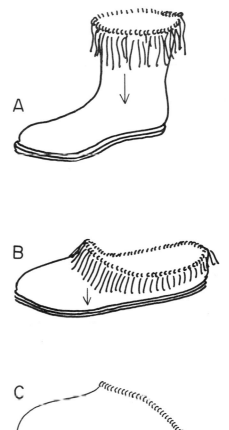

When more elaborate footwear is tied, it may be started by threading the working cords through the holes in the upper sole and tying the pattern with the cord ending as a fringe around the top. Be sure to trial fit this type of footwear frequently while shaping the top.

You may also begin footwear at the top by hitching the working cords over a starting support cord, working the pattern, and ending by passing the cords through the upper sole and gluing them as with sandals. A, B, C.

BOOK TWO

NAUTICAL FANCY ROPEWORK

TIED MATS

Mats are flat pieces of ropework used as coverings aboard ship. The old sailing vessels were made of materials subject to decay, rot, and corrosion, and the complex rigging of the older square-riggers had many points where spars, cordage, and sails would chafe if not suitably protected. Round braids (page 104), hitching (page 114), and the Turk's heads (page 58) were often used as protective wrappings for rails, spars, and rigging. Mats were similarly used where the surface to be covered was flat instead of cylindrical.

When made of hemp or cotton cord, mats also were excellent nonskid surfaces and were often used on deck in areas where sailors stood to work the lines. Below decks, mats covered the companionway ladders and passageways, providing nonslip footage while absorbing water that might otherwise rot unprotected wood.

The size and type of cord to use for any mat depends upon the intended use of the mat. One-inch hemp rope is excellent for a door mat, number 12 cotton seine twine for hot pads or coasters, and number 30 cotton seine twine for small mats to be applied as decoration to a lampshade or a small box. Regardless of the size of cord you are using, the principle of making tied mats is the same. For all mats, except the most simple, a tying board is a necessity, but the size and type of tying board is a function of the particular mat you are making. For mats up to a foot in greatest dimension, we use a small piece of corkboard and secure the cord with one-inch wire nails pushed into the board with the fingers. If you wish to use corkboard, get the higher grade of cork—that intended for use in bulletin boards—instead of the dark, coarse, crumbly cork being sold for decorative wall panels. This latter type of cork will not hold nails or pins securely and falls apart rapidly, continually dusting off small particles of cork. It also smells bad. Good substitutes for cork include acoustic ceiling panels, Cellotex, and Homasote wallboard. Check with a lumberyard or building supply dealer; they usually have a bin of scrap or broken panels and discontinued types of ceiling tile. If you get the acoustical tile, get the kind with a smooth surface, free from sound-deadening holes or rough texture. Either side of a smooth tile may be used, but a rough-surfaced tile should be used on the back only. Most of the materials we have mentioned may be easily cut to the desired shape at home with a hand saw or sharp knife. It is a good idea to have several tying boards on hand of assorted sizes. Two boards 6 inches by 8 inches, one 8 by 10, and one 12 by 12 would be a good start. With several boards, you don't have to finish one mat before beginning another one. If you have as many unfinished projects around the house as we do, you will appreciate the use for even more boards. More important, a mat begun for a specific use but which turns out midway to be not what you want, does not have to be taken apart or put aside in order to work on its replacement. We have a small box of mats tied up in idle hours with no specific use in mind and they are a good source of ready-made pieces for use from time to time. When making picture frames, for example, the corners are covered with mats that are usually tied in advance. If a particular set of mats intended for a frame doesn't look quite right, it is filed away and used later on another frame. Such a mat file is also an emergency source of coasters and hot pads.

For larger mats, particularly those made with heavy rope, it is necessary to use a larger, stouter tying board. A piece of half-inch plywood about 24 by 36 inches makes an excellent tying board for large mats, as well as for some of the larger square-knotted projects you may wish to undertake. You should be able to get a suitable piece of plywood at the lumberyard. Check around before you buy, however, because some yards still sell plywood only by the sheet, which is four by eight feet, and charge for each cut made in the sheet. A lumberyard catering to the do-it-yourselfer, however, should be able to provide the plywood cut to size at a significant saving. It is not necessary to get high-grade plywood for a tying board. Plywood is graded and priced according to the type and quality of the wood used to make it and the type of glue used to bond the wood. The wood is fir in the usual type of plywood and is graded A through D, according to the number of knots and defects in the surface layer of wood. Since each panel has two exposed sides, a two-letter code identifies the quality of the panel. Grade AA fir plywood is the best. We usually use CD plywood for tying boards. Tell the lumberyard that you would like half-inch or three-quarter-inch CD roof sheathing or flooring plywood, and you should be able to get several tying boards for about five dollars.

When using a plywood board, we secure the rope with 1½-inch common nails or brads driven about one third of their length into the wood. The nails may be removed easily after the project is completed, and the board reused indefinitely. Because of the size and weight of the plywood tying boards, it is not possible to carry them around with you to meetings, etc. but a small board, a container of nails, and a ball of twine fits easily into a carrying sack or a purse, and permits you to work on your mats in time otherwise wasted. It is possible to get a lot of mats done while the other PTA mothers are knitting or crocheting.

After you have a suitable tying board, place the nails according to the sketches accompanying each mat diagram in the section to follow. The nails will anchor your work in the early stages before the mat is stable, will help you keep the mat even, and will allow you to make several mats of the same design and size.

Each mat has a beginning point or points from which the cord starts on its serpentine course. When working from a ball or hank of twine, unwind enough to tie the mat, being very generous in your estimate. Do not cut the twine, because you will need more if your estimate of the cord required has been low. The free end of the twine is the working end, not the starting end. The mat is actually begun at the ball or hank of twine as is shown in the photograph. It is a good idea to saturate the working end with glue to prevent unraveling and facilitate its passage over and under the coils of the mat. After the working cord has made one complete passage through the pattern, it is taken through again and again to make the mats double-ply or triple-ply. With each passage of the cord, the spaces between the cords through which the working end must be threaded become smaller, so you may need a sailmaker's needle or small awl to open a passage for the cord.

Do not worry too much about getting the mat even or exact as you are tying it. It is better to tie the mat loosely

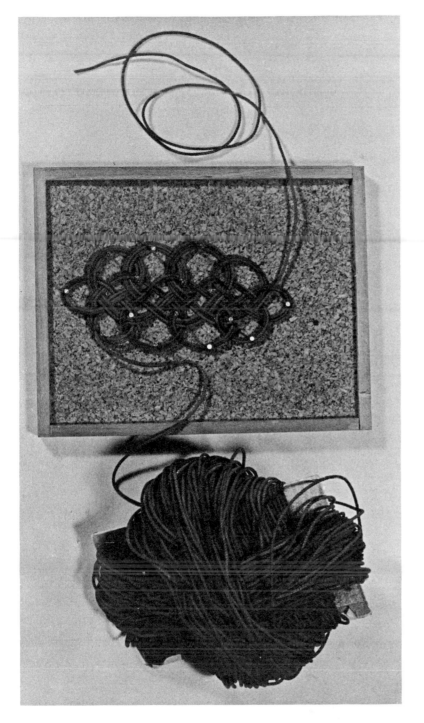

Method of organizing your work when tying ornamental mats.

and adjust it after it is off the board. Small mats may be adjusted in the hands by giving a tug here and there and taking up the slack by starting at the beginning and working through the pattern again. After the mat has been adjusted to your satisfaction, take the working and starting ends out on the back and trim. For mats that will not be reversible, the ends may be whipped and sewn or glued, but the best way to finish off the cord is to side splice the ends to the adjacent cord. A simple side splice is described in the section on splicing. It is not a difficult splice and will give your mat a professional appearance in addition to making it reversible. Doormats and hot pads are usually finished by splicing; we glue most of the others.

When the mat is to receive heavy use, we sew through adjacent coils using a sailmaking needle and heavy waxed linen thread. This sewing is nearly invisible and will hold the shape of the mat through the heaviest wear. If you wish to secure a heavy mat in this way, use a sewing awl or a sailmaker's needle and palm, as shown here. It may be difficult to find a sailmaker's palm, but try to locate one, for it is the best way to do the heavy sewing required in mats made of large rope. If you live near a port or in an area where sailing is popular, a marine supply house may stock palms.

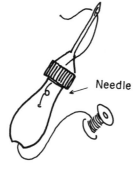

Needle

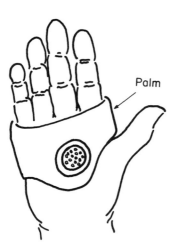

Palm

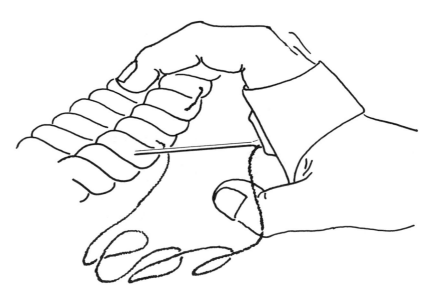

Sewing heavy rope mats together with the sailmaker's needle and palm.

Some of the mats we have chosen to present are made with a single cord, others with two. There are many hundreds of mat designs recorded in the various texts on ropework, and the complexity of some may be bewildering to the novice. Many are combinations or developments of basic patterns, and some use three or more cords to make the pattern. After you have experimented with the mats we will show you, you should be able to approach any mat pattern and figure out the method of tying it from a photograph or drawing. To find out the number of cords required to tie a particular mat, begin at any point and trace the chosen cord through all its loops and turns. If it traces the entire design before returning to the starting point, the mat may be tied with one cord. If it completes only part of the pattern, simply pick another point not included in the course of the first cord and trace it through the pattern. By repeating this procedure until the pattern is complete, you can determine any mat pattern.

In order for a mat to be stable, that is, in order that it not collapse when removed from the tying board, it must be completely interlocking. In other works, after the basic pattern has been traced through by the first passage of the cord, the cord will have been interwoven, crossing over and then under each successive cord it meets. When you refer to the diagrams of the mats to follow, notice that these crossings have been clearly shown, and be sure to pay close attention to them when tying the mats, for there is nothing more disheartening than watching your mat dissolve into a tangle of cord when removed from the board. Be careful when learning new mats from a reference book on matwork, because there are some ornamental mats used by tailors as trimming on uniforms included in these texts, and some of these uniform braids are unstable unless sewn to a backing. In all the books we have used so far, mats or braids that are unstable are clearly marked so in the text, but the worker who browses through a reference text picking new patterns from the pictures may run afoul of these unstable patterns. To check whether a pattern is stable, simply begin at an arbitrary point and follow the cord around. A pattern in which the cord goes over-under-over-under throughout the course of the mat will be stable. Mats in which the cord crosses over or under two or more cords may be stable, but it is more likely to be unstable. A few moments of checking a pattern before tying may save some grief later.

Suitably prepared with cord and tying board and aware of the pitfalls that await the incautious, you are now ready to begin making mats. As you will see, tied mats are very easy to make, and you could have tied several in the time it took to read the preceding section.

The first mat is an old friend, the *Round Carrick Bend Mat*. It is a simple mat that is useful for decoration and perhaps for coasters, but even when tied with large cord it is a fairly small mat. It is the Josephine knot in which the ends have been turned back into the knot. It is also a flattened three-part, three-turn Turk's head and may be tied around the fingers, according to the directions in the diagram on page 60, and then flattened out. This mat illustrates a problem with mats in general: one mat may have many names. Sometimes a mat may have different names because it may be tied in several ways, but more often the many names are based on the development of an identical pattern in several places or several navies. In the days before ready communication among nations, many knots, braids, and mats had several names. When designating a particular mat we have used the name that is most commonly found in the standard English texts on knotting and in some cases have used the name by which we first knew the pattern. If a large sailor wishes to call your mat by a different name, by all means defer to his opinion, for we can't be held responsible for differences of opinion arising from our choice of name for a mat.

There is a family of mats evolved from the carrick bend. The nearest relative to the basic round mat is the *Ocean Mat* shown in three stages on the opposite page. This mat is also known as the *Prolong Mat* because it may be tied as an extension of the round carrick bend mat. We have shown the latter method of tying it, because the principle of extending the basic mat may be used to further extend the prolong mat. The mat may also be tied by laying out the

Round carrick bend mat.

Stages in ocean mat (prolong mat).

tying board according to the last of the three diagrams. However long you make the prolong mat, it is always a series of interlocking carrick bends.

A second use of the carrick bend in mats is the basis of the figure-of-eight type of mat. In these mats, the design is made by isolated carrick bends (Josephine knots) tied in a series but not interlocking with each other. This type of carrick bend mat is called the *"Figure-of-Eight"* mat because of the resemblance of the Josephine knot to the numeral eight. These mats are quite distinct from the figure-of-eight *knot* presented on page 64.

The diagrams on this page show the round figure-of-eight mat with four knots. It is just a series of four Josephine knots tied flat in a closed circle. As in the ordinary carrick bend, two cords are used for each knot. This mat may be tied with any number of knots in it and the number chosen is determined by the desired diameter of the mat. The photographs of the finished work show several variations of this mat with different numbers of knots and different colors of cord.

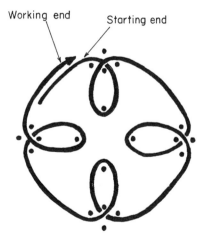

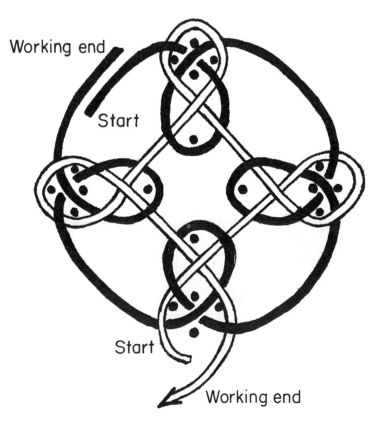

Steps in tying four-part round figure-of-eight or carrick bend mat.

The *Star Mat* is a close relative of the figure-of-eight mat in which the outer of the two cords used to tie it enters each knot from the center rather than from the outside. The star mat may be tied with any number of points, but is usually tied with five, at least in the United States Navy.

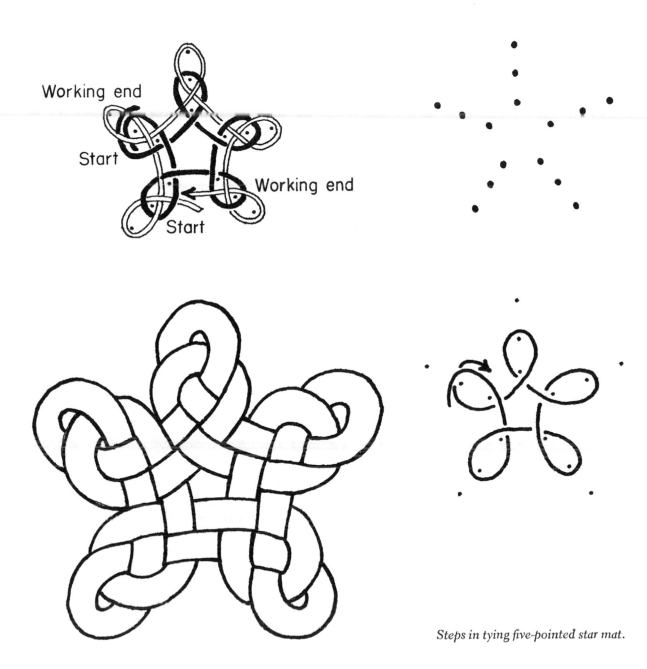

Steps in tying five-pointed star mat.

The *Square Figure-of-Eight Mat* with four knots shown here differs from the carrick bend mats presented above in that it is made with a single cord. Such a design represents a *tour de force* in geometry rather than a difference in the principle of tying carrick bend mats. Increasing the number of knots in this pattern is more complicated, and the interested person is referred to more advanced texts for other carrick bend designs tied with a single cord.

Steps in tying a square figure-of-eight mat of four parts made with a single cord.

The *Pretzel Mat* is shown in the diagram. The reason for its name is obvious. The three-part pretzel mat may be increased by adding more pretzels, being careful to interlock the additions in the same way as those in the illustration.

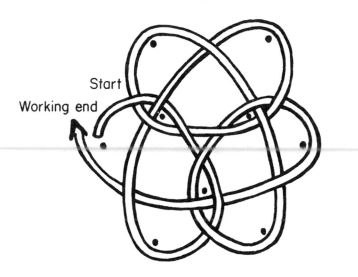

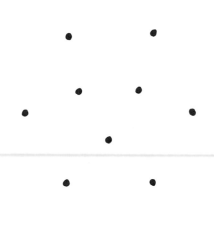

Pretzel mat.

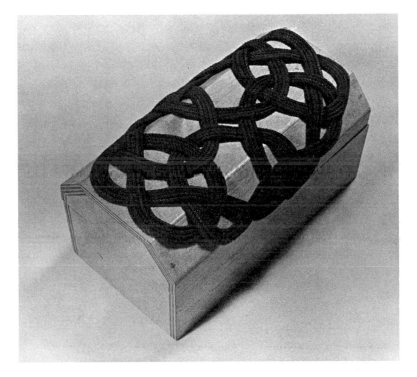

Six-part pretzel mat used on the top of a wooden purse. After the mat has been varnished, the rest of the box is decorated with other ornamental mats, braids, and fancy knots.

Flattened Turk's head of three parts and five turns.

The basic Turk's head, when flattened, became the round carrick bend mat. Other Turk's heads may be tied flat or flattened after tying to produce other mats. The flattened three-part, five-turn Turk's head is presented in the diagram. In the knot illustrated the cords have been tightened to bring the knot in toward the center. If the mat were tightened less, the center hole in the mat would be larger. The larger Turk's heads, when flattened, have larger holes in the middle. This fact limits the usefulness of the Turk's head for mats. When tied in combination with smaller round mats, flattened Turk's heads make good borders and may be sewn to the other mat, or both mats fastened to a supporting surface. The lampstand illustrated in the photograph below uses flattened Turk's heads on the bases.

Flattened Turk's head on base of lamp.

Three-part, five-turn Turk's head tied in a bowl. After the knot is completed, it is removed from the bowl and varnished to hold its shape.

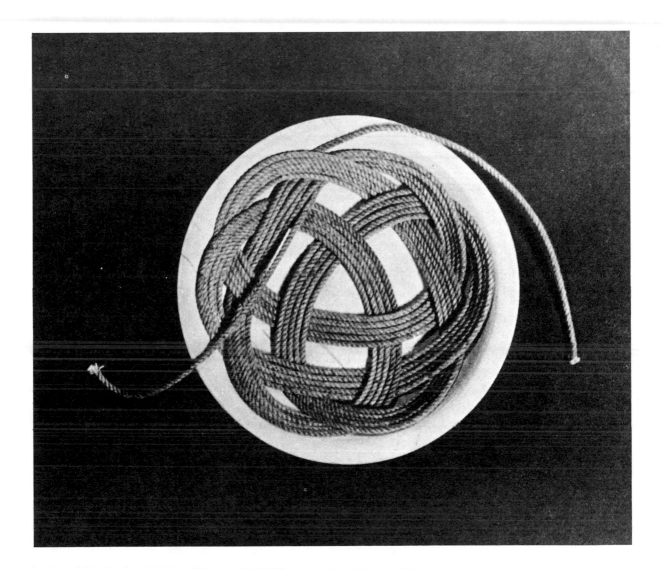

Other mats, which have become widely known and are commonly used by sailors in their designs, are illustrated on this page, (*Dragor Mat*); page 97, (*Cross Mat*); page 98, (*Hourglass Mat*); page 99, (*Six-Corner Mat*). The diagrams and photographs provided of these mats should be sufficient instruction for those who wish to make them.

Having mastered the few principles of tying mats, you should be able to make many other pleasing designs from any of the various knotting encyclopedias. The section on fancy applications will show a few of the many uses of tied mats.

Steps in tying dragor mat. This may be prolonged by increasing the number of loops on the sides.

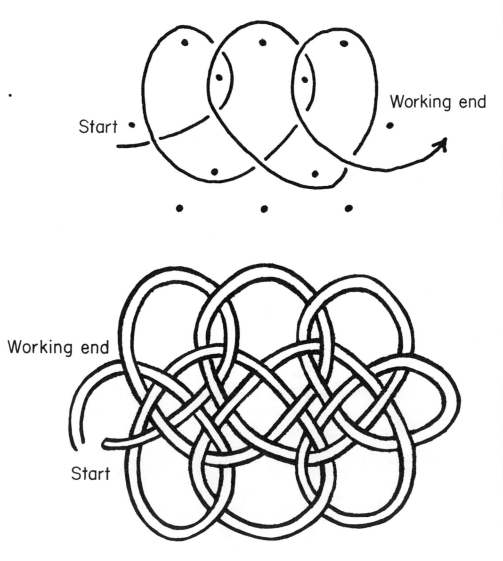

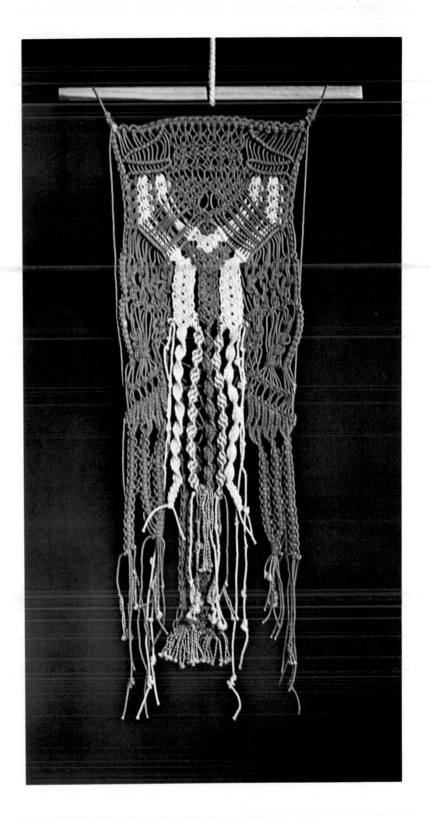

Wall hanging in gold and white cotton seine twine by Ellen Andes.

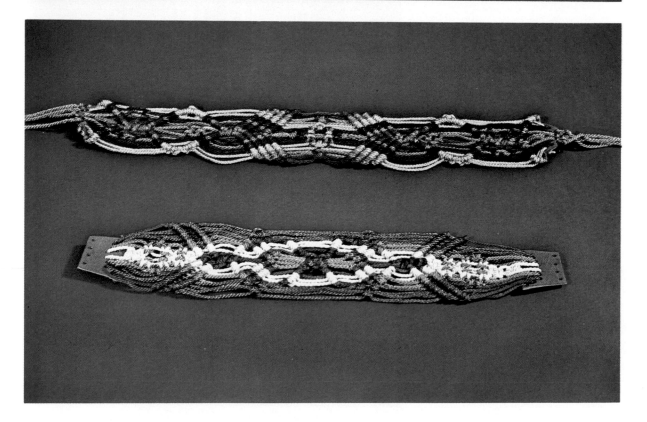

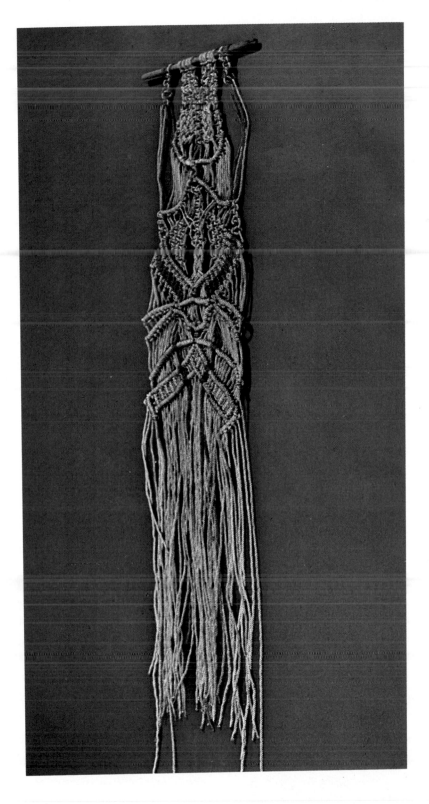

Macramé belts, wristbands and chokers made from a variety of fibers. (top left)

Nylon belts by Ellen Andes. (bottom left)

Wall hanging in nylon seine twine by Gene Andes. (right)

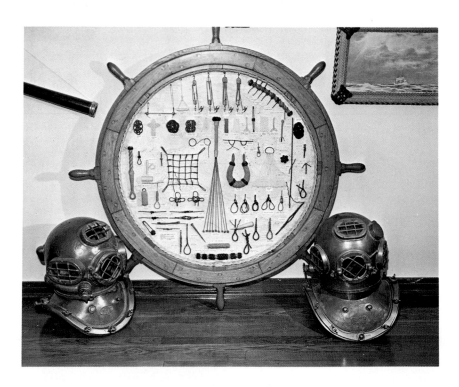

Ship's compass stand (top left) and bell stand (bottom left) with
decorative work. Some small projects made with braids and mats. (top right)
Ship's wheel knot board, illustrating working and ornamental knots
used by sailors. (bottom right)

Steps in tying a cross mat.

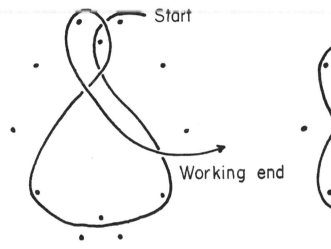

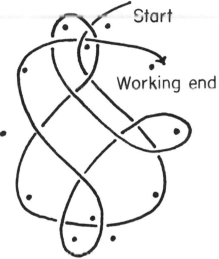

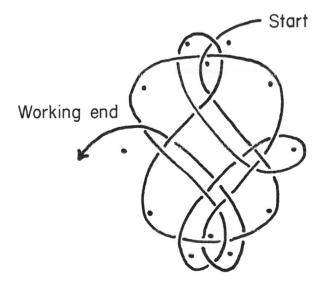

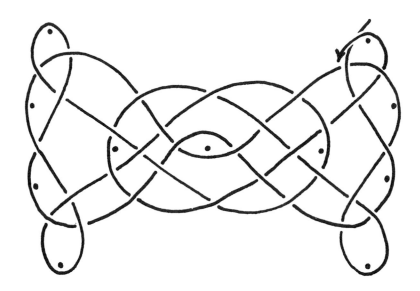

Hourglass mat.

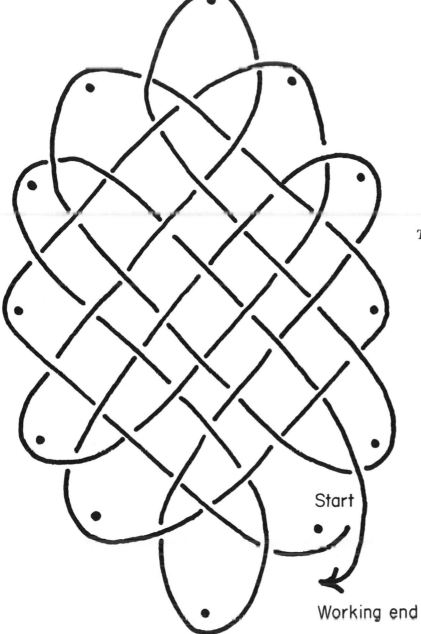

The six-corner mat.

Start

Working end

WOVEN MATS OR SWORD MATS

The *Sword Mat* was one of the most commonly used mats aboard ship. Although it is a woven mat, we feel its inclusion in a text on knotwork is justified by its wide use in nautical ropework and its beauty. Since sailing vessels did not carry looms, the equipment used by sailors to make the sword mat was improvised and crude. Limitations of equipment, however, did not prevent the development of complex and sophisticated patterns.

In weaving, the loom provides a frame upon which long threads are stretched (warp threads) through which other threads are woven (weft threads) to produce designs. The loom also includes heddles that raise and lower the

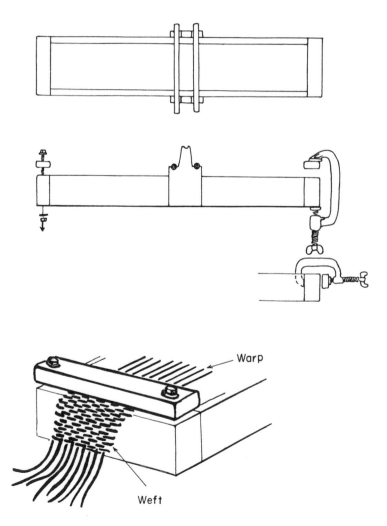

Modified sword mat tied around a pole. The weft (dark cord) goes over one and under four warp cords to make this pattern.

warp threads to make the separation, or shed, through which the weft threads are passed. I've included drawings of a simple loom which includes the basics: a frame upon which the warp is stretched, a means to advance the warp as the work progresses, and simple string heddles for the raising of certain warp threads when passing the weft across the work. In a loom such as the one illustrated, the weft is pressed back against the advancing border of the weaving with a coarse comb; better looms include a comblike heavy beater for the same purpose. Even the simple loom we have illustrated is far more than what the sailors used to make the sword mat.

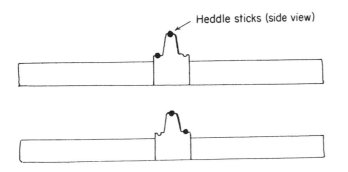

Heddle sticks (side view)

Simple loom. In this loom, the warp threads are clamped in place by bolts or C-clamps, and the warp is advanced when necessary by loosening and reclamping the warp. The string heddles shown are arranged for a plain weave (tabby weave), but many other heddle arrangements are possible.

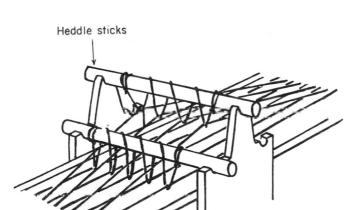

Heddle sticks

By most accounts, the warp was stretched between two sticks which were spaced apart a distance equal to the length of the desired mat, and the weaver moved along the mat as he worked. Some sailors undoubtedly rigged simple string heddles to every other warp cord, to produce the simple over-one-under-one pattern of the plain or tabby weave, but for narrow mats of short length, it is likely that a long sailmaker's needle was used to thread the weft through the warp cords. This latter method allowed the weaver to vary the pattern without rerigging the heddles. By passing the weft over two and under two, over two and under one, over three and under one, and so on, the sailors produced many different woven mats. On these pages I've shown what equipment the sailors may have used to make the sword mat, some of the pattern variations possible.

When the sailors used their crude weaving equipment a thin stick of wood, or perhaps the flat of a sword blade, was used to beat back the weft after each pass. It is from the resemblance of the sailor's beater to a sword, or the use of a sword as a beater, that this mat derives its name.

Since its length is limited only by the distance you have to rig the warp, and the width is limited only by the length of the weavers arms and patience, the sword mat was found very useful for long nonskid mats. The edges of the finished mat were generally bound by oversewing or tying fringe with warp threads. We use the sword mat for making long strips of mat for covering boxes and picture frames.

Six sword mat variations.

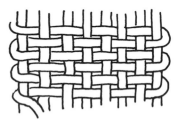

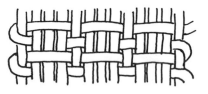

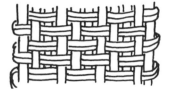

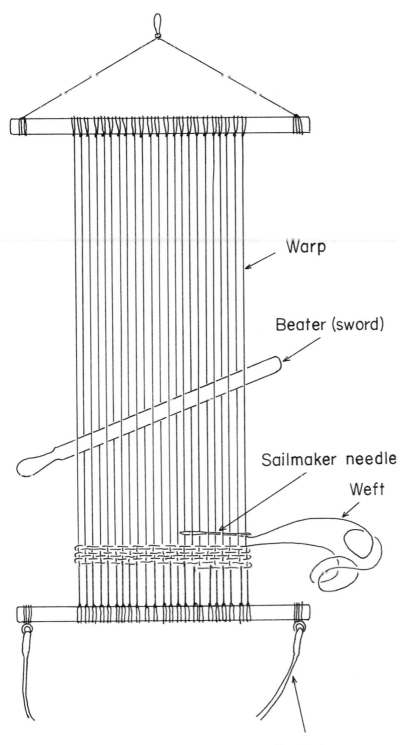

Warp

Beater (sword)

Sailmaker needle

Weft

Backstrap

Sword mats
used on a picture frame.

A backstrap loom such as may
have been used by sailors to
make the sword mat.

BRAIDING

The simplest of braids is the three-part common braid called flat sennit or pigtail braid. It is probably known to almost all of you, but for those without a sister who wore braids, we have included in this diagram instructions for making it. The principle of the pigtail braid is common to all flat sennits regardless of the number of strands used to make them. Common braids almost always have an uneven number of strands—three, five, seven, nine, and so on. As shown in the photographs, each strand may be multiple cords, and when such a braid is made the cords are held flat so that they will lie side by side in the finished braid. This is different from the braiding of hair in which the multiple strands of hair are not held flat.

To begin a *common braid,* divide the strands into two unequal groups with the larger group held in the right hand. For a five-part braid, there would be two strands in the left hand and three in the right, as illustrated below. Pass the

Common braiding.

Left: three-part common braid.

Right: five-part common braid.

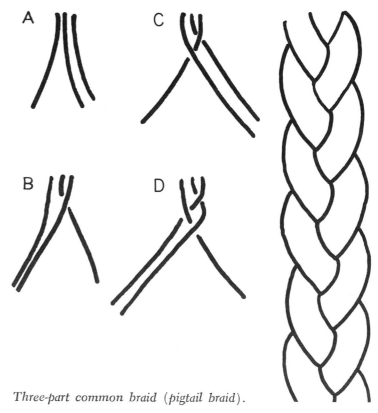

Three-part common braid (pigtail braid).

uppermost cord on the right in front of the other right-hand cords to the center and add it to the cords of the left group as shown in the diagram. There are now three strands on the left and two on the right. Pass the uppermost strand of the left hand group in front of the other cords on the left and add it to the right hand group. Repeat these two steps for the desired length of braid. As you work, the ends of the cords being braided will tend to tangle, so you must frequently untangle them.

The principle of common braiding may now be stated in general terms: Use an uneven number of working strands; divide the working strands into two groups of cord with the larger group held in the right hand. Braid by passing the uppermost strand of the larger group in front of the other strands in the group and adding it to the smaller group. The smaller group is thus increased to the larger and the process repeated.

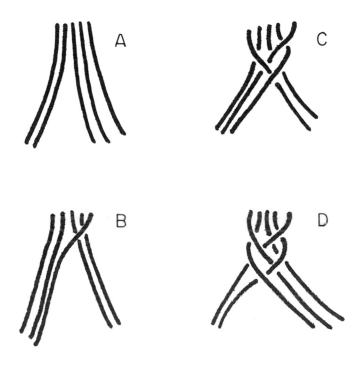

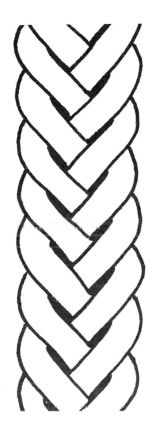

Five-part common braid.

This form of braiding may be used with an even number of working parts, but the resulting braid will be asymmetrical. If you wish an asymmetrical braid for some ornamental application, try a braid with four parts. Divide the cords into groups of three and one, as shown.

If the braid you wish to make is to be used without a supporting structure, as in a belt or purse shoulder strap, braids of more than five or seven parts are not practical because they will be easily deformed. Common braids of greater numbers of parts are very useful, however, for applications where they will be cemented to some supporting structure such as a picture frame, table, or tray.

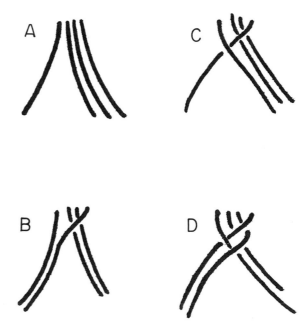

Asymmetric four-part common braid.

The *French Sennit* is a close relative of the common braid. Unlike the common braid, when worked with an even number of strands it produces a symmetric pattern.

To make the French sennit, begin with an uneven number of strands and divide the strands into two groups of cords with the larger group held in the right hand. The uppermost cord of the right hand will again pass to the center and be added to the left-hand group, but instead of crossing the other cords of the right-hand group in front, it weaves under and over them. The five-part French sennit is diagramed, the first pass of the right-hand cord takes it under and then over the other right-hand cords.

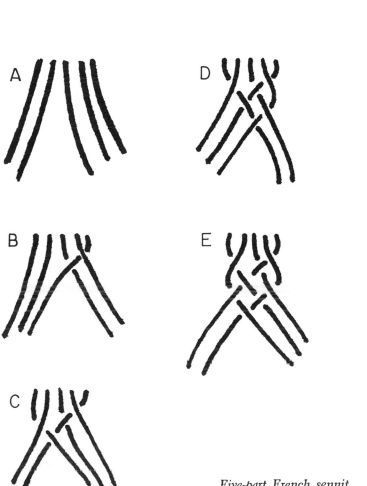

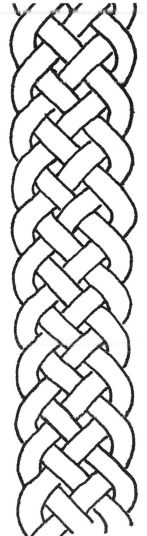

Five-part French sennit.

When worked with an even number of strands, the principle of the French sennit is the same and is shown in the diagram of a six-part sennit.

A common variation of the French sennit is one similar to the latter type of common braid discussed above. One cord is held in the right hand and the remaining cords are held in the left. In this version, the right-most cord is always the one used and is woven under and over all of the other strands, ending on the left edge instead of the center. This braid is illustrated in the diagram and in the photographs on the opposite page.

After you have mastered the French sennit and have learned to handle multiple strands of cord when tying braids, you will find it easy to make variations on the braiding by using different patterns of weaving than the simple under one over one of the basic French sennit. For example, try passing the working strand over two under two, or over two and under one.

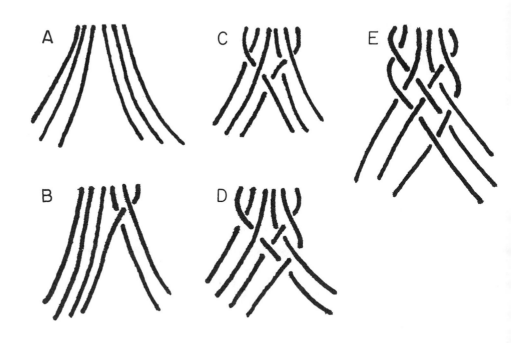

Six-part French sennit.

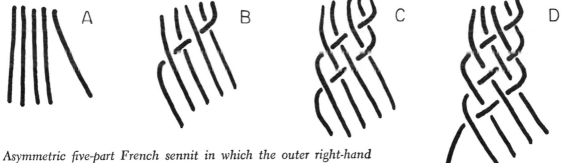

Asymmetric five-part French sennit in which the outer right-hand cord is always the one worked.

Modified French sennit in which the right cord is the one woven through the other strands.

Braiding variant of the French sennit in which each cord passed over two and under two strands.

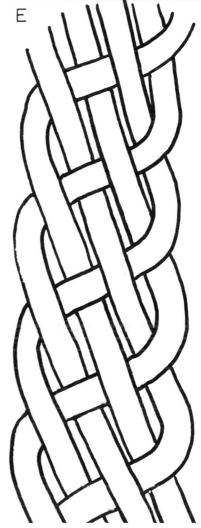

If you wish to learn other braids, you will find adequate examples of braiding in several of the encyclopedias of knotwork. Remember that braids may be indexed under their specific names, or as sennits, plats, or braids.

The braids we have considered so far are all flat braids. There are also round, square, and hollow braids. These vary in complexity but, in general, are more difficult to do than flat braiding. *Round and square braids* are made with an even number of strands; a minimum of four is required for the simplest. The basic four-part sennit is either round or square depending on the tension applied during the braiding and how the braid is molded with the fingers after completion. The four-part square braid is presented here and in the diagram opposite. The principle of this braiding is that

French sennits with even numbers of working strands

Left: Four-part French sennit.
Right: Six-part French sennit.

the uppermost strand is passed around behind all the other strands, between the two strands of the opposite pair, and ended on the same side it started but below the other strand of its own pair. This process is then repeated with the next uppermost strand, which will be of the opposite pair. To make the braid round, roll it between your hands. To make it square, pound it gently with a mallet, shoe, or block of wood. Also notice the effect of different color arrangements of the cords.

The eight-strand square sennit is probably the most commonly used square or round braid. When tied as we will show you, it is square. When tied over a core of rope or fibers, it is round, and, indeed, it is the basic braid used in making braided rope. To begin, divide the eight strands into two

Four-part round or square braid.

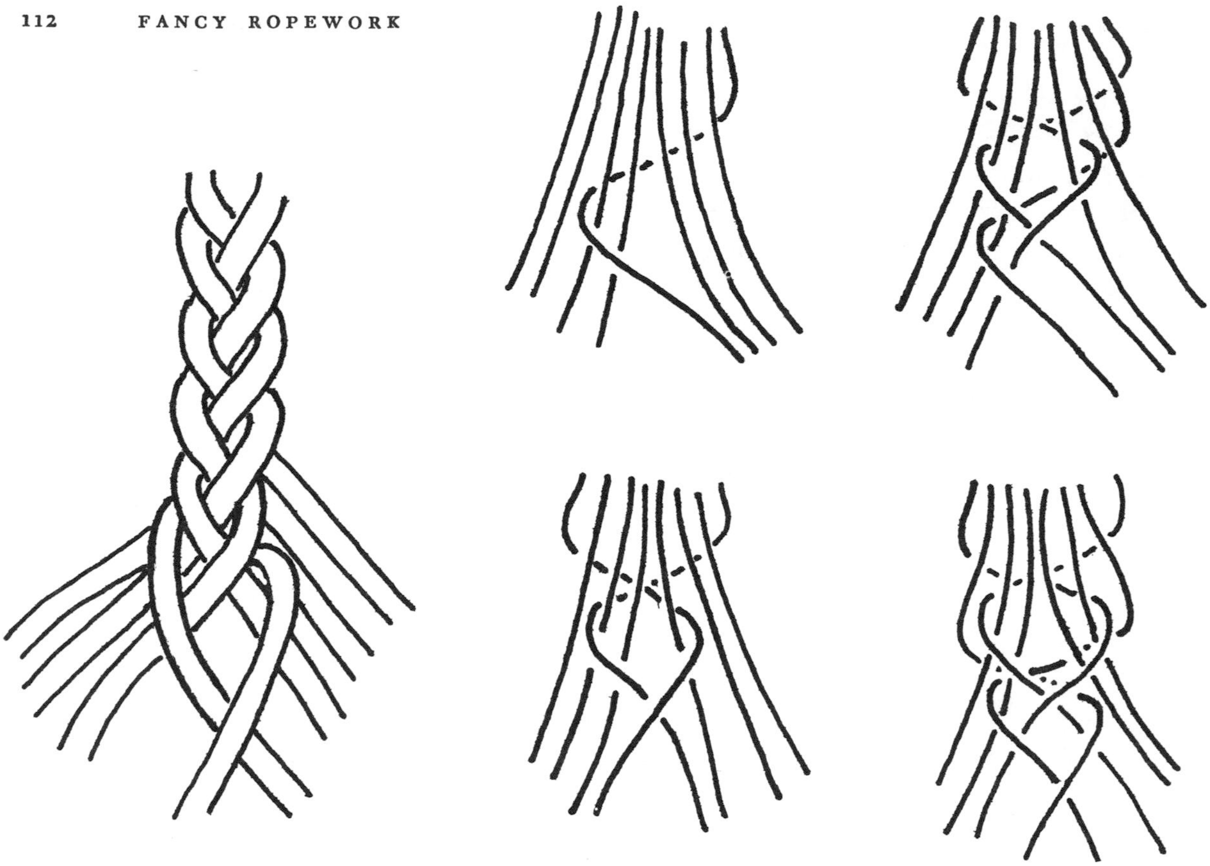

Eight-part round or square braid.

groups of four. Pass the upper left cord behind the other strands of the left-hand group out to the front between the center two strands of the right-hand group, and back to the left-hand group of strands where it becomes the lowermost strand of the group. See the diagrams. Proceed similarly with the uppermost strand of the right-hand group, as shown in the diagram, and continue to work the braid by alternating working cords from each side in turn.

Square braids of greater numbers of strands may be made but are not as attractive as the eight-strand square braid, and they tend to lose their shape. When tied as round braids over a core of wood or rope, they will be quite handsome, however. Round braids of more than eight strands tend to be tubular and thus easily deformed, so that some core is actually required for stability. Round braiding of more than eight strands done over a core using multiple cords in each strand is often termed "coachwhipping." Round braiding done over a tapering core of rope is called "cross pointing." Whatever the name, the principle of the braiding remains the same.

The interested reader is referred to any of the knotting encyclopedias for further information about braiding.

Coachwhipping (round braiding of more than eight strands done over a round support).

HITCHING

A "hitch" for our purposes may be defined as a loop of cord passed around some supporting structure. Known to the sailors as a "bight" and also termed a half hitch, the simple loop is shown in the diagram and is the basis of a series of patterns of hitching used as decorative and protective coverings for ropes, rails, and other objects subjected to hard wear aboard ship. There are many patterns of hitching devised by sailors, who called the process "coxcombing," but with few exceptions the patterns are simply combinations of half hitches tied with single or multiple strands of cord.

The simplest form of hitching is made with a *Single Cord* hitching repeatedly around the support. This is the basic

The half hitch

Simple half hitch patterns. The left-hand pattern has been allowed to spiral following the natural tendency of the pattern, and the middle pattern has been pulled back to align the knots in a straight row. On the right, reversing the direction of the working cord after each interlocking hitch has been made.

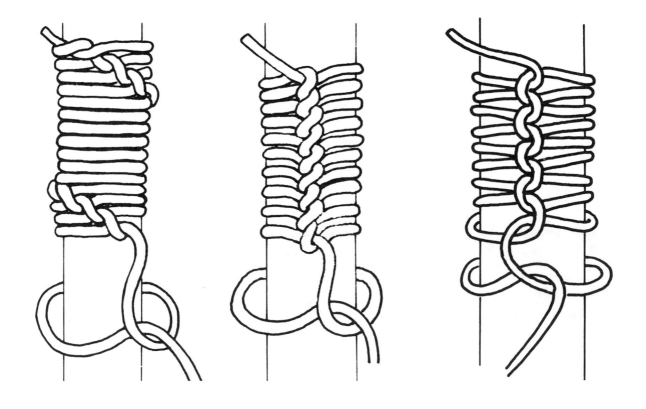

pattern in which the cord continues around the support in the same direction tying one half hitch in each turn. Even this most simple of patterns has two versions. In the first, each successive hitch falls just to the side of the preceding one, following the natural tendency of the rope to align in this way. In the second version, the cord is pulled smartly back after each hitch is made so that the knots lie in a straight line rather than in the spiral formed by the former version.

If the direction of the cord is reversed after each hitch is formed, you may produce another variation of the same basic hitching pattern.

More Than One Cord may be used in simple hitching. Passing two strands around a support in the same direction produces the patterns shown in the diagram on this page. In the first pattern illustrated, the knots formed by the two cords lie just under each other and form a double spiral. In the second pattern illustrated, the knots of each strand have been on opposite sides of the support so that the resulting pattern has two separate spirals.

Example of reversing the direction of the working cord.

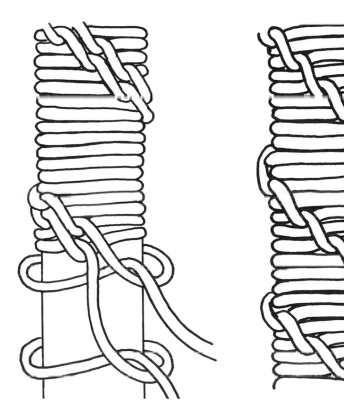

Simple hitching with two cords spiraling in the same direction with the hitches being made right below each other.

The same pattern as in the preceding diagram except that the spirals of each cord have been separated.

There is another type of covering knot related to the above called *Fender Hitching*. In this form of hitching, the article to be covered is generally large as when making a fender—a large pad used to protect the sides of a vessel when docking or upon the approach of a careless yachtsman. In this type of hitching, the hitching cords do not encircle the object to be covered because the large diameter of the object makes this impractical, but rather hitch over other cords running around the object at right angles to the direction of the hitching cords. The second cord, which forms the actual support for the hitching, may be a separate cord that spirals down around the article to be covered, or may be the preceding row of hitching, both shown in the diagrams here. In the former case, there are usually many vertical cords hitched over the support cord as it spirals around the object to be covered. Notice that the hitches may be tied overhand or underhand, as in the diagram. In the second type, which is known most widely as the fender hitch, the working end of the cord is usually passed through the loops of the row above with the aid of a large needle or a marlin spike or fid.

Fender hitching is still much used to make bumper pads and fenders for ships and boats of all sizes. Usually a simple canvas bag is made and filled with cotton padding, spun yarn, or kapok, and the protective hitching applied to the outside of the canvas being stoutly sewn to the bag at the top and the bottom. Two or three fenders would make a handsome and welcome present for any friend with a boat. Any of the hitching described above is also suited for covering lamps, bottles, or table legs.

Underhand and overhand hitching used as a fender covering.

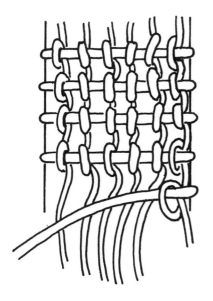

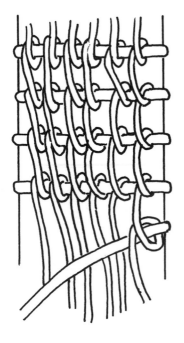

The fender hitch. Each hitch passes through the loop of a hitch in the row above.

Splicing was an essential skill aboard a sailing vessel with its miles of rope requiring constant repair and replacement during a voyage. Every hand and officer aboard a vessel knew how to splice quickly and well because such knowledge was not uncommonly a matter of survival. The towering masts and huge spars of the wood sailing vessel were entirely supported and positioned by the fine webs of rope which appear so frail. Because the fibers used to make rope during the sailing era decayed rapidly when exposed to the elements and the strains imposed on them, the sailor spent much of his time at sea inspecting, repairing, and replacing the rope upon which the safety and efficiency of the ship depended.

The rigging of a sailing vessel was divided roughly into two classes. Standing rigging was the cordage that formed the static supports for the masts and certain other equipment. Large shrouds passed around the tops of each section of the masts and led down to the sides of the vessel where they were fastened to large metal plates bolted to stout timbers in the sides of the vessel. The smaller diameter ratlines were clove-hitched to the shrouds in ladderlike fashion to form the means for the sailors to climb up the masts to work the sails. In addition to the shrouds, which provided lateral support, there were stays, termed fore- and backstays, that led down from the tops of each section of each mast to fasten to adjacent masts or special timbers placed in the ship for that purpose. In the early days of rigging design, it was common practice to lead stays from one mast to another so that the several masts of a vessel were mutually dependent. It was soon discovered, however, that a warship which lost one mast to the cannon fire of an opponent, lost all her masts, and the battle. Before long, it became standard practice to design the standing rigging in such a way that each section of each mast was supported independently of its neighbors. In practice, this meant that long stays led down from the tops of the masts to timbers in the decks designed to receive them. The tremendous amounts of force to which the stays were subjected required that the ropes used be strong. Unfortunately, the only way to increase the strength of twisted hempen cordage is to make it thicker.

SPLICING

Before the development of metal cordage and the synthetic fibers widely used today, the thickness of rope required for such applications had made further increases in diameter of the ropes impractical. The rope used for standing rigging was too thick to be tied into knots, so it was fastened by splicing. The techniques used to protect these important ropes from wear and weather were many and were constantly being altered throughout the history of the sailing vessel. The problems of preserving natural fiber cordage were never really solved, and most vessels had the rigging replaced at regular intervals. Until the decline of the sailing vessel and the development of metal cordage, most standing rigging was rot-proofed by being painted with tar and covered at points of wear by wrappings of cloth and smaller diameter rope. It is the coat of tar that gave the standing rigging its characteristic black color.

Running rigging was that portion of the rigging which was dynamic, in constant change as it was used to position the spars and sails. This rigging was of smaller diameter than the standing rigging and relied on multiple pully systems for the mechanical advantage needed to alter the positions of sails and spars. Because running rigging ran through pulleys and because tar would foul pulleys, it was not possible to effectively rot-proof the running rigging. Running rigging was, therefore, constantly being renewed and repaired as it deteriorated. Whenever possible, rope aboard ship was repaired, since the amount of new rope a ship carried was necessarily limited. Aboard a warship, as much space as possible was devoted to arms and munitions. Aboard a merchant ship, cargo had the priority where space was concerned. By the time provisions for the crew, for as long as two years, were aboard, there was precious little space even for essential supplies. Rope was extremely valuable, therefore, and never discarded. Damaged rope was repaired, for such repair required little more than hand labor, and the sailor spent many hours repairing rope.

A rope that has broken may be joined with a knot. But a knot will not pass through a pulley. And a knot is actually a weak spot in a rope. Even the simplest of knots reverses and kinks the fibers of the ropes, and the best knots are only about 40 per cent as strong as the unknotted rope. Joining a rope by a splice, however, produces a joint about 80 per cent as strong as the rope. Splicing may be done in such a way that the diameter of the rope is not increased, and the rope can pass through a pulley. Splicing was a skill as essential to the development of sailing as that of rope-making.

Most people regard splicing as extremely difficult, and with the development of newer longer-lasting cordage, the general knowledge of splicing has greatly decreased. Splicing is simple. If you should ever doubt your ability to learn splicing, remember that even the most dull-witted sailor, born and raised in an age of general lack of education, could do many splices. If he could, you can.

Our presentation of splicing will be restricted to the splicing of three-ply twisted cord. Although it is possible to splice metal rope and braided synthetic cords, the techniques are quite different and require special equipment. After you have mastered the simple splices we will show you, you may refer to an advanced text on splicing if you wish to learn any of the other techniques.

The principle of a splice is that the ropes to be joined are unlaid for a distance and the component cords of each rope are then sewn or woven through the intact portion of the other rope. The important thing about a splice is that the fibers of the rope do not kink or reverse direction. The splice holds because when pull is applied to the rope, the coils tend to tighten and thus clamp the interwoven spliced cords even tighter. The greater the pull on the rope, the greater the force with which the interwoven spliced cords are gripped.

For twisted rope, then, there is really only one basic type of splice. All the many names given to specific splices refer to the particular way in which the splice was made, which, in turn, depends upon the intended application of the spliced rope. The tools required for splicing depend upon the nature of the rope to be spliced. For splicing cotton seine twine, we find a large pin or hemostat and an upholsterer's or sailmaker's needle useful.

When splicing stout hemp cord, it is necessary to use a wood peg, called a fid (see Glossary), to open the coils of rope

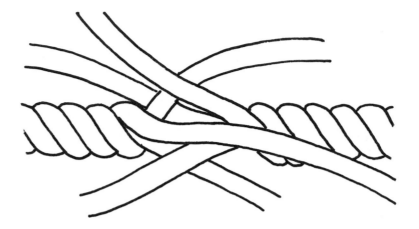

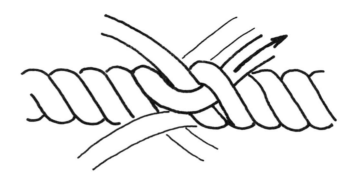

The short splice. Each of the unlaid cords is interwoven over and under the cords of the unlaid portion of the other rope.

to pass the splicing cords through. On large cable or rope, it may be necessary to use a mallet to pound the fid through the rope, but it is unlikely that you will have to resort to any such measures if you are splicing twine.

The *Short Splice* is used for joining two ropes end to end. It is made by unlaying the ropes for a distance of 7 times the diameter and placing the ropes end to end so that the unlaid cords interdigitate, as shown on this page. One cord at a time is then passed over and under one of the coils of the other rope, passing around the rope in a spiral opposite to the lay of the rope. After each of the three cords has been thus passed, the process is repeated. At least three passes are necessary on each side for the splice to hold, and four is better. The splice is finished by trimming the ends of the cords close and in some cases by whipping the ends. This splice creates a bulge in the line where the repair was made. If the rope must pass through a pulley this bulge might foul the line. When a bulge in the line is undesirable, the sailor uses a long splice.

In the *Long Splice*, the ropes to be joined are unlaid for a distance of 20 diameters and placed end to end as for the short splice. The cords are not immediately interwoven through the coils of the intact rope, however, but are carefully spiraled around the rope in the channel between the coils, as shown. The cords are thus wound around the intact rope for a distance of 10 to 15 diameters, and the fibers in each cord are gradually trimmed as the winding proceeds so that each winding cord tapers to about half its original diameter. Then the cords are woven through the coils of the intact rope in a manner similar to that used for the short splice, except that the weaving cord passes around in the same direction as the lay of the rope instead of opposite it as in the short splice. The long splice is finished similarly to the short splice, and sometimes the entire length of the splice is wrapped and whipped.

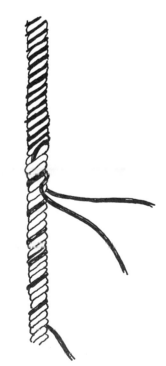

*The long splice is used when the rope to be joined is to be
of uniform diameter without the bulge formed by a short splice.
It has little application in fancywork.*

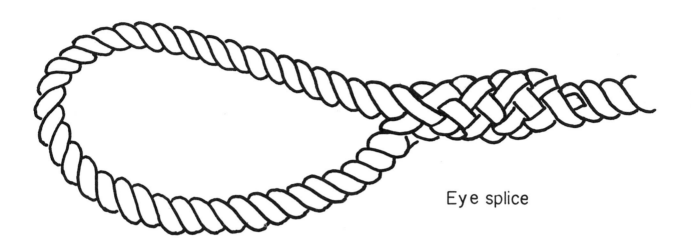

Eye splice

Stopper knot (man knot).

The *Side Splice, Back Splice,* and *Eye Splice* are simple applications of the short splice and are shown in the diagrams above. In the back splice, the cords are usually reversed by tying a stopper knot before making the splice.

After rope has been unlaid, the component cords may be used to tie knots or be recombined in different ways to make other rope. It is not our intention to discuss here such techniques, but we feel that a brief presentation of the stopper knots is in order.

A *stopper knot* is a knot tied with the component cords of a rope, usually at the end, to prevent the rope from running completely through a pulley or through a hole.

We will present only the *Man Knot,* probably the most

Side splice   Back splice

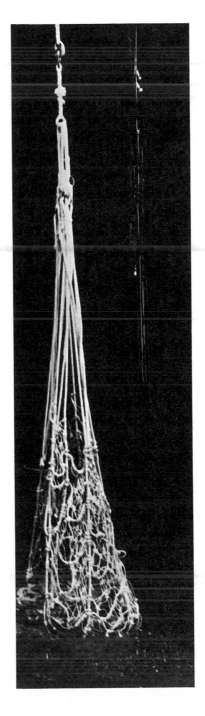

commonly used stopper knot, and the interested person is referred to the texts on splicing of the knotting encyclopedias for further examples.

The combination of the wall knot and the crown knot produces a man knot. See pages 124 and 125. The two knots are very simple and are best learned from the diagrams. Tie the wall knot then the crown knot and follow each around a second or third time and you will have a handsome stopper knot called the man knot, useful for ending cords in a macramé hanging, making buttons, or purse clasps. The knot is generally finished by passing the cords down through the knot and trimming them close or using them to make a short back splice.

Child's swing and wall hanging in natural cotton cord by Gene Andes.

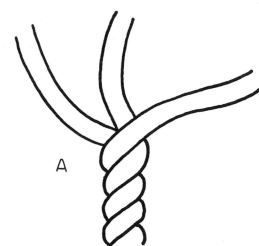

A

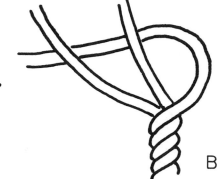

B

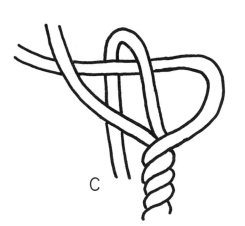

C

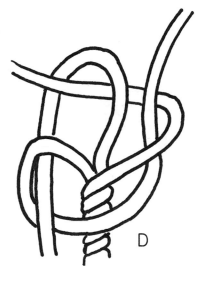

D

Wall knot.

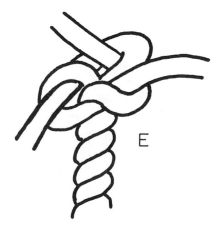

E

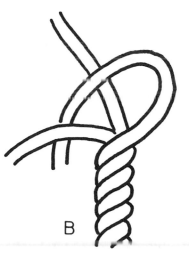

A

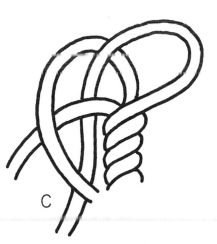

B

Crown knot.

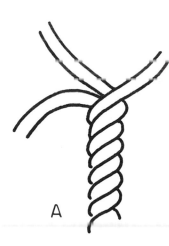

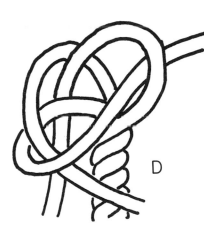

D

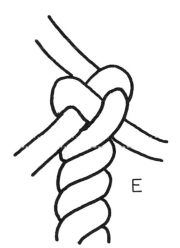

C

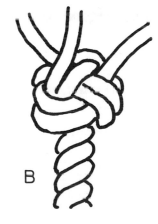

E

The man knot is a wall knot followed by a crown knot and then doubled. The knot is finished by passing the cords down through the center of the knot and trimming close.

A. Wall knot and crown knot.
B. Wall knot portion doubled.
C. Completed knot.

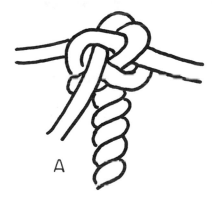

A

B

C

After some practice with the simple splicing described, you will have gained some insight into the nature and working characteristics of twisted cordage. The three cords of an unlaid rope tend to retain their spiral if the rope is unlaid carefully, and they may be retwisted into rope again. From time to time, you may want to unlay part of a rope or a cord, tie a pattern with the component cords, and then reconstruct the rope or cord. The diagram on opposite page shows simple planters constructed by this means. The large tassel on the one planter was made by unlaying the rope completely, back to the yarns, and then proceeding as described earlier for tassel making (page 63).

The sailors' comb cleaners were long tassels made by unlaying Manila hemp rope. The slight residual waviness of the unlaid yarn makes this sort of tassel very decorative.

Cringles are closed circles of rope without apparent seam and make fine purse handles or rings for circular hangings. To make a cringle, unlay a rope of length equal to three times the circumference of the cringle plus several inches. Use one of the cords of the rope to twist the cringle, as shown. Finish by tucking the working ends, as in a long splice.

Unlaying rope to make different decorative tassels.

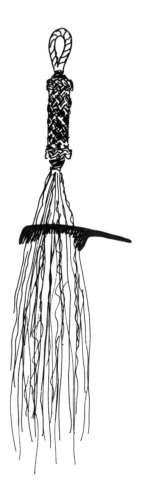

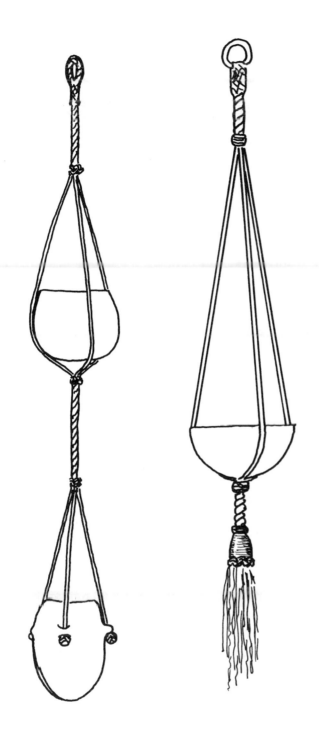

Suggestions for hanging candles or planters using splicing, stopper knots, sennits, tassels, and other fancy ropework.

A rope cringle.

FANCY APPLICATIONS

Because the current rediscovery of fancy ropework focused mainly on square knotting, or macramé, nearly any of the currently available books on macramé will contain examples of recent trends in square knotting. Some of the current books are better than others, and we consider Harvey's *Macramé*, Andes' *Practical Macramé*, and Meilach's *Macramé* to be of merit and worthy of including in a home library on knotting. Since most of you already have been exposed to many examples of square knotting, and since we already have outlined an approach to self-instruction in macramé in the earlier part of this book, we will not include further discussion of square knot design. Although the usefulness of the nautical fancywork presented in the preceding chapters is to some extent readily apparent, we will provide some suggestions about how you may use the new techniques you have learned.

Most of the patterns we have shown you were designed and used as coverings. Some may be used without support, as when making hot pads or coasters from tied mats, but most will be tied onto a support or secured to some support after tying. The sword mat and the tied mats are the only mats commonly used without support.

Perhaps the simplest project using mats is the decoration of a small box with some of the tied mats or braids. Lay out the tying board so that the mat you tie will be the proper size for the box on which it is to be mounted, tie the mat in the usual fashion, secure the ends on the underside with glue, and then glue the mat to the box with Duco Cement or white glue. Be careful that the glue does not get onto the top of the mat, or the mat will take varnish irregularly. During the twenty or thirty minutes that the glue requires to dry, frequently press the coils of the cord firmly down onto the box, align the adjacent coils of cord and make any final adjustments in the position of the mat. Tied mats and braids may be glued to the sides and edges of the box, but remember that a braid will have a seam where it is joined, and this seam should be placed inconspicuously or covered by a tied mat glued onto the braid at the seam. For larger boxes you may fashion handles from large cord by tying stopper knots in the ends and fastening the cord to the box with loops of cord or Turk's heads.

Working sketch for a decorated box using sword mat, Turk's head, tied mats, and stopper knots.

The illustration is just an example of the many ways to cover boxes with mats and braids. Note that stopper knots make fine feet for boxes and may be used to make a rope clasp. After the box has been suitably adorned, the ropework should be thoroughly varnished, at least six coats being required. After the varnish has completely dried, the boxes will be extremely durable and may be cleaned with a stiff brush or soap and water, when dirty. If you leave the ropework unvarnished, it will collect dust and soil with time, so it is better to varnish. By using cord of different colors, applying mats and braids to painted boxes, or "antiquing" the ropework with wood stain as described above, you can produce many handsome projects in very short order.

When decorating circular boxes or covering such things as tin cans, a seamless three-part braid is made by using the Turk's head to encircle the piece. Multi-ply Turk's heads with cords of contrasting colors were used to tie the knots around the circular box in the photograph. Square knotting can also be used to cover a box as illustrated.

We have made a number of tables and stands covered with ropework and find them quite handsome. They are also quite inexpensive. To make a small coffee table, you need only a piece of half-inch or three-quarter-inch thickness having one good side (AC plywood) and a set of the readily available bolt-on tapered table legs. The top surface of the table should be smooth so we don't cover it with ropework, but glue a nautical print or a piece of nautical print fabric or canvas to the plywood with white glue and varnish the top thoroughly with polyurethane plastic varnish, sanding well between coats. If you wish to glue a print to a table top, use white glue, diluted one to one with water, and moisten the print well before gluing to avoid crinkling of the paper. Wheat-base wallpaper paste and a wallpaper brush can also be used to glue a print to the plywood. After the top has been varnished, we glue braids around the edge of the wood. If a thick edge is desired, we glue wood strips around the edge of the plywood to support the braid edges. Press the braids firmly to the wood as the glue dries and varnish them well. Unless the corners have been rounded, we usually seam the braids at each corner, because braids will

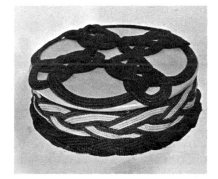

Round wood box covered with figure-of-eight mat and Turk's heads.

Square knot box covering.

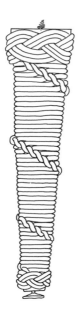

Table leg covered with simple hitching and Turk's heads top and bottom.

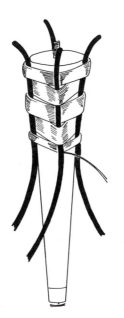

Weaving a covering for a table leg on the leg itself.

kink and deform if carried around a sharp corner. Small tied mats at each corner cover the seams in the braids.

The legs are mounted to the under side of the table with small plates that screw into the wood of the table top. To mount the plates, be sure to use screws shorter than the thickness of the plywood lest the tips of the screws come through the top of the table. Some of the plates have two-leg positions for angled or straight legs. We prefer straight legs because the ropework looks better. After the braid and mats have been varnished, we cover the legs with any of the hitching patterns described earlier and place a Turk's head at the top and bottom of each leg. The legs are varnished and fitted to the table by screwing them into the plates on the bottom of the table.

The first diagram shows the appearance of a finished leg ready for mounting. In the second diagram we show a simple variation of weaving that is a sort of tubular sword mat useful for covering table legs.

The table which supports the bell stand (shown in color) was specially constructed to carry the weight of the brass bell and the bell frame, which is heavy galvanized steel pipe. The table top is one-inch plywood and the legs are two-by-fours securely braced. Such heavy construction is rarely necessary in furniture, but you could use lighter lumber to make your own table legs if you wished. Despite the size of the lumber used in the bell stand, it is not ponderous because of careful attention to proportion and the delicate effect of the rope covering. There are several detail photographs of this stand which show how hitching and braiding was used to cover the tubular steel of the frame and how the Turk's head was used to brace and tie together parts of the frame. In reality, the side braces of the frame were welded to the vertical frame members, but in the finished piece, the Turk's heads appear to hold the frame together. As usual, tied mats were applied here and there to cover seams and bolts.

Floor lamps, pole lamps, and stands made of round pipe are easily decorated with round braids, hitching, and Turk's heads. By tying short segments of hitching or braiding separated by Turk's heads, it is possible to work with relatively short lengths of cord, just enough for each section, since the ends of the old and new cords are hidden by the Turk's heads. When covering a long section of pipe with the same braid you will have to work with long cords and will spend as much time untangling cord as tying. If the pipe you are covering is of uniform diameter throughout its length and you want to thicken the column near the base of the top, build up the pipe by wrapping with scrap cord before covering with braid. We purchased a floor lamp for fifty cents at a junk store, cleaned and rewired it, and then covered it with ropework. The base was decorated with a circular figure-of-eight mat with six parts after being wrapped with cord. Because the heat generated by the large bulb was enough to warm the metal around the socket, we built the ropework out away from the bulb base about one inch by tying over a coffee can. The switch handle was then extended through the can and decorated with rope, as pictured. If you decorate a lamp, be sure to check that the heat from the bulb will not be excessive because varnished cord will char and burn if sufficiently heated. If you are in doubt, have an appliance serviceman check the lamp for you or use a low-wattage bulb.

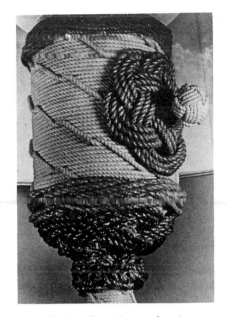

Detail of a floor lamp showing hitching, Turk's heads and mat work around the bulb socket.

Lamp base covered with fancy ropework.

Other cylindrical objects that may be covered with rope-work include glasses, mugs, and bottles. Coxcombing and fender hitching are particularly attractive for covering fancy bottles for use as decanters or as bases for table lamps. When hitching over a tapering support, such as a bottle, begin at the smaller end so that the advancing column of hitching will be self-supporting. Turk's heads and various tied mats are often applied for further ornamentation.

Rope-covered picture frames have been made for years by sailors, and there are many surviving examples to be found in marine museums and water-front bars. Many frames we have seen appear to have been made more to show the sailor's skill in knotting than to attractively frame a picture. The more ornate frames produced, particularly in the Victorian era, certainly detract from the pictures they enclose, and they are gaudy by today's standards. Picture frames need not be overdone, however, and the frames illustrated do not de-

Fancy ropework picture frame.

tract from their pictures, but enhance them. Rope frames for seascapes and pictures of sailing vessels are particularly appropriate and make a handsome appearance in an informal room decorated in nautical style.

The frame to be covered with ropework must be a simple one, homemade if you wish, with rounded edges and corners and a minimum of fluting or decorative carving. We get our frames at the dime store and prepare them by rounding and reinforcing the corners and filling any irregularities or carving in the wood with wood putty. Beginning with the inner edge of the frame, successive partially overlapping layers of braids and woven mats are firmly glued to the face of the frame, being careful to align the braids and press them firmly onto the wood. The corner seams on the face of the frame are mitered. The outer edges of the frame are covered with a continuous strip of braid which can pass the rounded corners without kinking. As this outer braid is glued and nailed to the frame, it is pressed down firmly so that it molds around the edge of the frame and meets the braids applied to the face of the frame. If necessary, the space between the braids on the face and the edge braid is covered by another layer of braid. Tied mats cover the corner seams in the edge braid and the braids on the face of the frame. Thorough varnishing will further secure the braids to each other and to the frame and will prevent deforming of the inner braid that slightly overlaps the picture. Because of the ropework and the varnish, these frames are extremely strong and will last indefinitely.

There are many, many other uses for the various nautical fancywork patterns you have learned. Small oval or round tied mats become hair barrettes by passing a small stick or dowel through them. Braids or ornamental cord may be used as curtain tiebacks, sashes, or trim on clothing. A tied mat may be glued to a belt buckle, and cords may be threaded through holes in leather and used to tie ornamental knots on belts or leather garments. Using a simple rope-making machine, we have made rope of silver wire and used it to tie a Turk's head ring. There is no limit to the uses of fancy ropework; in a short time you should be able to surpass our own small beginning.

Detail of picture frame.

GLOSSARY

Back splice A splice made in the end of a rope by reversing the direction of the cords and short splicing them through the unlaid portion of the rope. See page 123.

Basket weave A variation of the alternating square-knot pattern in which every other horizontal row of knots is replaced by simple weaving of the cords. The basket weave may be made double or triple by weaving two or three rows between each row of square knots. See page 42.

Belay To secure a rope to a cleat or belaying pin by passing it around both ends of the cleat or pin several times and finishing with a figure-of-eight knot.

Bend To join two ropes end to end with a knot. The knot used to join two ropes is a bend or a bending knot. (Carrick bend.) Also, to fasten a rope to some support, as to bend a rope to a spar or anchor.

Bight An unsupported loop or sag in a cord, as between two parts of a knot or between two knots.

Block

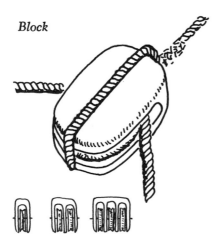

Block A wood-enclosed pulley for changing the direction of a rope in a ship's rigging or used in combination with another block to multiply the pulling power of the rope.

Braid, braiding Interweaving of cords in a particular way to produce flat, round, or square pieces with length much greater than width. See page 104.

Braided rope (yacht braid) Rope in which the outer surface is a tubular braid of eight or more parts over an inner cord of straight fibers. Braided rope is commonly made of cotton, nylon, or dacron braid covering a core of cotton, nylon, dacron, or steel. Many of the popular ornamental cords sold for decorative knotwork are braided cordage incorporating multiple colors or metallic fibers in the outer braid. See page 17.

Cable Heavy cordage with a direction of spiral opposite to that of rope. When viewed from the side, cable-laid cord has a spiral from upper right to lower left. Cable was usually made by twisting together several ropes and was intended for heavy use as anchor cable, towing lines, or the like.

Cable-laid

Cable laid (left laid) A descriptive term for twisted cordage in which the spiral of the component cords is opposite that in rope. When viewed from the side, the cords will pass from upper right to lower left.

Carrick bend

Carrick bend (Josephine knot, wake knot) A knot used to tie two ropes together end to end. This knot is the basis of many of the ornamental ropework patterns popular among sailors. See page 58.

Clove hitch (also called double half hitch) Two half hitches of the same handedness tied adjacently on the same support. See page 44.

Clove hitch

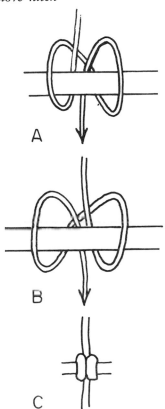

Coachwhipping Round braiding of more than eight cords done over some round support. See page 113.

Cord Hard, twisted yarns or cords.

Coxcombing A general term for hitching. See page 114.

Cross pointing Round braiding used to cover a tapering section of rope. As the braid is made the number of cords in the braid is gradually decreased to accommodate the reduction in diameter of the support.

Crown knot A knot tied with three or more cords in which each cord passes downward through a loop in an adjacent cord. This knot is most commonly used to reverse the direction of the cords in an unlaid rope when making a back splice or tying a stopper knot. See page 125.

Eye splice   The formation of a loop in the end of a rope by leading the end of the rope back and side splicing to itself. See page 122.

Fairlead   A wood board or thimble (see Thimble) with a hole in it serving as a guide through which a rope is passed.

Fancy knot   A knot, practical or decorative, that is used in a particular application more for its appearance than for its strength, ease of tying, etc.

Fancywork   The sailor's term for decorative knotting. This type of knotting included projects that were only ornamental. It also made items of daily use aboard ship more attractive by special knotting techniques.

Fid

Fid   A conical wooden wedge used to open spaces between the coils of a rope when splicing.

Figure-of-eight knot

Figure-of-eight knot   A knot used similarly to the overhand knot. See page 64.

Half hitch   A turn around a support. It may be made left-handed or right-handed. See page 114.

Half hitch

Half knot   A non-specific term used by some to mean either the left-hand or right-hand part of a macramé square knot and by others to mean a half hitch. Better to avoid using this term.

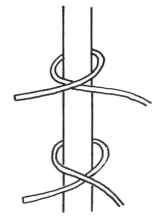

Hawser   A rope-laid rope of large diameter used to tie up a vessel or to tow another vessel. Mooring lines are usually hawsers. (See Cable.)

Hitching   The covering of some supporting rope or rod by tying half hitches in various combinations. See page 114.

Josephine knot   See Carrick bend. (Glossary)

Lark's head (also called *two half hitches*)   Two half-hitches of opposite handedness tied adjacently on a support. See page 38.

Lay   The characteristic spiral of a twisted cord. Also, to twist together cords or yarns into rope.

Lead   The direction of a rope in rigging or in a knot. Also, to pass the working end of a rope through a knot.

Long splice   See page 121.

Macramé   Originally synonymous with square knotting, this term is now taken to mean fancy ropework in general.

Man knot   A popular stopper knot made by tying a wall knot surmounted by a crown knot and then following each cord through the knots again. The knot is finished by passing the cords down through the knot and cutting them close or back splicing with them. See page 125.

Manila   The sailor's term for Manila-hemp rope, the rope used most commonly aboard United States vessels until comparatively recently.

Marlinespike (marlingspike)   A long tapering metal cone used similarly to a fid.

Mat   Any flat piece of ropework. Mats may be tied, woven, or braided. See pages 82, 100, 104.

Overhand knot (also called *simple hitch* or *simple knot*)   A simple knot tied in a line to prevent unraveling or to make a temporary stopper knot. See page 65.

Overhand wrap knot   A variation of the overhand knot in which the working end is tucked repeatedly through the loop of the knot in order to increase the size of the knot. See page 64.

Lark's head

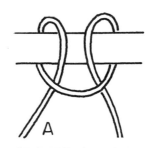

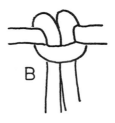

Marlinespike

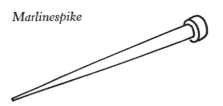

Overhand knot

Plat   Flat braid. See page 104.

Ply   The number of strands in a twisted rope, or the number of passes in an ornamental knot. Most rope is three ply; most tied mats are made three or four ply.

Pear knot   A cord tied in a line by layering several figure-of-eight knots before making the final tuck through the lower loop to lock the knot. Its uses are similar to those of the overhand wrap knot. See page 65.

Ratlines   Small diameter ropes tied across the shrouds of a vessel to provide means for the crew to ascend the masts.

Rope   Cord built up to the desired diameter by twisting together the desired number of yarns and cords with the last twist being in a counterclockwise direction. Rope will have a spiral from upper left to lower right when viewed from the side.

Rope-laid

Rope laid (plain laid, right laid)   A term describing the direction of the spiral in twisted cordage. Rope-laid cordage has a spiral from upper left to lower right when viewed from the side.

Running rigging   That portion of a sailing vessel's rigging that worked the sails and other equipment. Running rigging passed through multiple pulleys and was not rot-proofed with tar as was the standing rigging.

Sailor's lace   Fancywork applied to certain portions of a vessel usually only on special occasions, as the decoration of a ship's boat when it would be used to bring aboard an important person.

Sennit, sinnet, or sennet   A long narrow strip of rope work, usually braided or square-knotted. See pages 47, 104.

Short splice   See page 120.

Shrouds   Large ropes used to provide lateral support for the masts of a vessel.

Side splice   Joining the end of one rope to the side of another by means of a short splice. See page 123.

Smartly   To tie, place, and tighten a knot exactly and speedily.

Soft laid   Loosely twisted cordage.

Spar   Any of the wooden or metal beams or rods that supported the sails of a vessel, exclusive of the masts. Spars included yardarms, booms, and bowsprits, and each had a different name based on the sail it carried and its position on the ship.

Spin   To make yarn from fibers by twisting.

Splice   To join two ropes, usually end to end, by interweaving the ends of one rope between the coils of the other. In a splice, the cords do not reverse direction as in a knot, and splicing is thus the strongest repair that can be made to a cut or broken rope. See page 118.

Spun yarn   Yarn hand spun from fibers salvaged from old rope.

Square knot   A knot used to bend two ropes together. It is tied in two parts as illustrated. If only one of the parts is tied twice, the knot is a granny. A sound knot may be tied by making the two parts in either order shown. Also, the basic knot in macramé, which is usually tied by using two cords to tie a square knot over two other cords that support the knot. It also may be tied by making the two parts in either order, but requires both parts for the knot to be stable. We term the knot left-handed or right-handed according to which cord crosses in front of the support cords in the first part tied. See page 40.

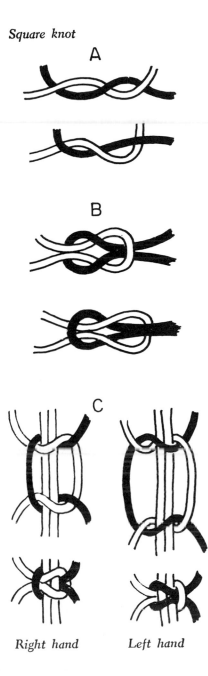

Square knot

A

B

C

Right hand   *Left hand*

Square knotting The sailor's term for projects knotted using only a few of the many knots they knew: the square knot, the clove hitch, and the lark's head. Many fine examples of old square knotting survive in private collections and marine museums.

Standing end The beginning end of the rope used to tie a knot that does not pass through the knot but remains in its starting position.

Standing rigging That portion of the rigging of a sailing vessel supporting the masts and other equipment. Standing rigging required only infrequent adjustment during a voyage, and any adjustments were made without passing the ropes through pulleys, so standing rigging could be rot-proofed by coating with tar and wrapping with tar-saturated cloth and cord.

Stays Large ropes supporting the masts of a vessel in fore and aft direction.

Thimble

Stopper knot Any knot tied in a rope to increase its diameter at that point to prevent its running through a pulley, fairlead, or other hole. See man knot page 125.

Strand In a rope, one of the component cords from which the rope has been twisted.

Sword mat A woven mat. See page 100.

Thimble A doughnut-shaped metal fairlead with a groove around the outside permitting its attachment to the rigging with a rope eye spliced around it.

Top The uppermost portion of a mast. Mast height was increased by doubling together multiple masts, so the particular top was denoted by naming the mast to which it belonged. Also, one of the small platforms built at the doubling of the masts to support the rigging of the upper of the doubled masts, and in warships to accommodate armed men who could fire at the crew of an opposing vessel from this elevated vantage point.

Turk's head Any of a family of knots in which a single cord circles repeatedly around a cylindrical support interlocking with itself to produce a closed circular braid. Instructions for a simple Turk's head of three parts are given on page 59.

Unlay To untwist a twisted cord.

Wake knot The heraldric term for the carrick bend.

Wall knot A knot tied with three or more cords by passing each cord upward through a loop made in the adjacent cord. This knot may be tied by passing the cords through the loops to the left or to the right, but when tied with the unlaid cords of a rope the direction of tying the knot must be the same as the direction of spiral of the rope. See page 124.

Whipping Wrapping of small diameter cord or yarn applied to the cut end of a rope to prevent unraveling.

Working end In knot tying, the end of the rope, or ropes, that is used to actually tie the knot.

Wrap knot See overhand wrap knot. See page 65.

Yarn A number of fibers twisted together.

Whipping

BIBLIOGRAPHY

ENCYCLOPEDIAS

The Ashley Book of Knots, Clifford W. Ashley, Doubleday & Co., Inc., Garden City, New York, 1944.

Systematic coverage of knots and related lore of the sea, excellent reference work for the experienced knotter and fine reading, but some of the drawings are difficult to follow unless experienced.

Encyclopedia of Knots and Fancy Ropework, Raoul Graumont and John Hensel, Cornell Maritime Press, Cambridge, Maryland, 1952.

Complete listing of knots and braiding, explanations of many knots are sketchy and some photographs are not clear, but still an excellent book for the advanced knotter.

RECOMMENDED BOOKS ON MACRAMÉ

Square Knot Handicraft Guide, Raoul Graumont and Elmer Wenstrom, Cornell Maritime Press, distributed by Random House, Inc.

Macramé: The Art of Creative Knotting, Virginia I. Harvey, Van Nostrand Reinhold Company, New York, 1967.

P. C. Herwig Co. Square-knot pamphlets; a series of instructional pamphlets for the beginner to intermediate level knotter.

Macramé: Creative Design in Knotting, Dona P. Meilach, Crown Publishing Co., New York, 1970.

Practical Macramé, Eugene Andes, Von Nostrand Reinhold Company, New York, 1971.

OTHER BOOKS ON MACRAMÉ

Step-by-Step Macramé, Mary W. Phillips, Golden Press, New York, 1970.

Macramé, Imelda Pesch, Sterling Publishing Co., New York, 1970.

P. C. Herwig Co., 264 Clinton Street, Brooklyn, New York 11201.
Wide selection of natural and dyed cord, macramé accessories, and instructional pamphlets.

The Sun Shop, 7722 Maple Street, New Orleans, Louisiana 70118.
Dyed and undyed nylon and cotton seine twine at reasonable prices, assorted macramé cords in cotton, jute, and nylon in colors, many types of wood, glass, and ceramic beads, brass buckles and hardware, custom-made buckles, custom-dyeing service, books and macramé kits.

LaNasa Hardware Co., 1027 Decatur Street, New Orleans, Louisiana 70116.
Undyed cotton and nylon seine twine, braided nylon cord in all sizes, nylon rope, marine hardware.

Craft Yarns of Rhode Island, Inc., P. O. Box 385, Pawtucket, Rhode Island 02862.
Good selection of weaving yarns and macramé cords in wide range of colors.

Lily Mills Co., Shelby, North Carolina 28150.
Weaving supply house that carries a good selection of macramé cord.

Frederick J. Fawcett, Inc., 129 South Street, Boston, Massachusetts 02111.
Weaving supply house with some yarn and cord suitable for macramé.